Secure Relationships

Secure Relationships

Nurturing Infant/Toddler Attachment
in Early Care Settings

Alice Sterling Honig

An NAEYC Comprehensive Membership Benefit

National Association for the Education of Young Children
Washington, D.C.

Photographs copyright © by

Hildegard Adler: 11
Nancy P. Alexander: 22, 25
CLEO: front cover (top), 16, 18, 32, 56
Ellen Galinsky: 49
Bill Geiger: 34, 37
Jean-Claude LeJeune: back cover

Jonathan Meyers: front cover (bottom), 5, 29, 42, 45
Katherine Nell: 8
Marilyn Nolt: 47
Subjects & Predicates: 10, 26, 44, 48, 53
Renaud Thomas: 3, 55
Christina Tolomei: 6

National Association for the Education of Young Children
1509 16th Street, NW
Washington, DC 20036-1426
202-232-8777 or 800-424-2460
www.naeyc.org

Through its publications program the National Association for the Education of Young Children (NAEYC) provides a forum for discussion of major issues and ideas in the early childhood field, with the hope of provoking thought and promoting professional growth. The views expressed or implied are not necessarily those of the Association. NAEYC thanks the author, who donated much time and effort to develop this book as a contribution to the profession.

Library of Congress Control Number: 2002101885
ISBN 1-928896-03-0
NAEYC #123

Publications editor: Carol Copple
Editor: Catherine Cauman
Editorial assistance: Natalie Cavanagh
Design and production: Malini Dominey

Printed in the United States of America

About the Author

Alice Sterling Honig, Ph.D., is professor emerita of child development at Syracuse University and a licensed New York State therapist. She has published hundreds of journal articles and book chapters as well as taught courses on child care, parenting, language, prosocial and moral development, observation and assessment, cross-cultural childrearing, theories of child development, and research methods and problems in child development. Among her books are *Talking with Your Baby: Family as the First School* (with H. Brophy); *Infant Caregiving: A Design for Training* (with J.R. Lally); *Parent Involvement in Early Childhood Education; Risk Factors in Infancy; Prosocial Development in Children: Caring, Helping, and Cooperating* (with D. Wittmer); *Optimizing Early Child Care and Education;* and *Behavior Guidance for Infants and Toddlers.* Every June (for 26 years) she directs the annual national Quality Infant/Toddler Caregiving Workshop at Syracuse University. Dr. Honig has been honored by Syracuse University with the Chancellor's Citation for Academic Excellence and by Onondaga County with the award of Woman of Achievement in Child Development.

Contents

Introduction

Maija wanders restlessly around the toddler classroom, touching and poking at toys, knocking some blocks off a table. When her special caregiver, Ms. Genia, comes back from her break and calls out a cheerful greeting to her, Maija looks up and makes a beeline for her, wrapping herself around the provider's legs. Once safely in her teacher's arms, Maija sighs contentedly and relaxes, resting her head on Ms. Genia's shoulder. Her teacher suggests that they read a book together, and Maija babbles excitedly, pointing to the bookshelf. After choosing a favorite book, Maija settles onto her teacher's lap, pops her thumb into her mouth, and looks on with interested, bright eyes as Ms. Genia shares the pictures and words with her.

By her positive greeting, her desire to snuggle with her caregiver, her acceptance of the adult's hugs, and her compliance with the suggestion for reading together, Maija shows her deep confidence in her teacher's ability to comfort and care for her and help her focus her attention and settle into a cozy learning experience.

Child care providers and teachers of infants, toddlers, and preschoolers hear a lot about attachment and how important it is for children's emotional well-being. But some teachers feel that attachment issues are the exclusive domain of families. Others see that children behave in puzzling or worrisome ways in the classroom or family child care home but do not relate the behaviors to attachment difficulties. As a caregiver, you may be aware of how much the interaction styles of young children are influenced by their early attachments to their parents. And you may well have noticed that how a particular young child behaves with you and with peers in the classroom seems related to the child's affectionate attachment to you. Evidence of secure attachment to caregivers (discussed in Chapter 1) can be clearly seen in child care settings.

> *Tamar is lovingly attached to Mr. Brown, her caregiver for the first two years at the child care center. When she is moved to a group of preschoolers in the fall, Tamar has a hard time adjusting. When Mr. Brown comes to visit her in her new classroom during his break, she looks angry and runs away from him. The center staff think they have given Tamar a proud step up in life by moving her in with a preschooler group. But Tamar is not prepared for this change from the secure, loving world of her infant/toddler classroom. She interprets the move as a sign of Mr. Brown's rejection of her.*

Tamar's reproachful behavior when Mr. Brown comes to visit her helps the teachers become aware of how powerful a young child's attachment to a caregiver can be. Staff need to consider children's feelings carefully when they move them to a new group or transfer caregivers from one group to another. Helping young children with new emotional and social adjustments means caregivers and teachers must take into account the emotional relationships infants and toddlers have built with them. Because transition times can be traumatic and stressful for young children, one way to promote easier transitions is to move children *with their friends* to a new classroom.

When a caregiver works hard to build a child's secure attachment to her, she can count on the power of that emotional bond to increase the child's cooperation with her requests.

> *Full of energy and playfulness, 2½-year-old Will snatches the eyeglasses from a student observer visiting his toddler classroom. When the student asks him to give back her glasses, Will just grins and crawls under a table. From across the room Will's teacher, busy with another toddler, surveys the scene. "Will, honey," she calls out, "please give Ms. Kay's glasses back to her. She needs them to read her papers. Thank you, Will." The toddler reluctantly but promptly returns the student's glasses to her. His secure positive attachment to his caregiver helps him activate the self-control needed to comply with her request.*

Secure attachments early in life are the keystone for ensuring children's mental health (Honig 1984). When we emphasize the caregiver's role as strongly as the role of mentor or teacher in furthering a child's emotional well-being, building secure attachments can be considered a prime goal in early childhood education.

This book addresses aspects of attachment that every caregiver needs to understand to become more adept at the challenging work of nurturing early positive mental health in young children. It offers suggestions for enhancing your skills in nourishing each child's secure relationship with you in the child care setting. Many of these ideas affirm the loving, tuned-in interactions you already carry out. Your special responsive attentiveness to the needs and tempos of the very young are very important—a crucial filament in the emotional lifeline of secure attachment.

Data supporting the importance of such skills are provided by theory, research over the past decades, and clinical evidence across developmental stages and across cultures (Honig 2000a). Careful observation forms the basis of most attachment research. But checklists and analytical tools such as the Ainsworth Strange Situation procedure (discussed in Chapter 1) and the Waters Q-Sort technique[1] are used as well.

Why is attachment so important for us to know about and be deeply concerned about in the lives of the babies and young children we serve? Why does it matter so much that we warmly, actively, and intentionally, in our daily routines and innumerable tiny gestures of kindness and empathy, build secure attachments between children and ourselves? The children will move on to other age groups and classes. Some parents will feel jealous of any loving relationship their child has with a teacher. So why do we owe this priceless gift to each child we serve—the gift of secure attachment to a nurturing caregiver?

Research and clinical findings over the past decades confirm the connection to later emotional well-being of a secure attachment between each baby or young child and a warm, stable adult. Behavioral styles and intimate interactions throughout people's lives are shaped by the core patterns of their early relationships. Intergenerational research, cross-cultural research, and developmental research following infants from the first year through adulthood have shown us the later importance of early attachment:

• Older toddlers who had been assessed as securely attached in infancy were far more likely in a stressful learning situation to approach challenging tasks with enthusiasm and try to problem solve rather than give up or become angry and upset. They were also more compliant with their mothers' helpful suggestions than were children who had been assessed as insecurely attached. Early loving was tied to later ability to tackle harder learning problems.

• Infancy attachment classifications have been related in significant ways to later preschool social competence (Turner 1991). Pairs of secure preschoolers playing together were observed to be more harmonious, less controlling, more responsive, and happier in their play than secure-insecure pairs. More often they peacefully negotiated a fair settlement of differences; complied with one another's requests and suggestions during play; and endorsed their play partners' preferences rather than insist on their own way. Insecure avoidant infants were often characterized later in the preschool classroom as bullies with their peers. Insecure ambivalent children in preschool sometimes behaved as victims and had trouble with peer interactions (Troy & Sroufe 1987).

• When 11-year-olds from stressful, low-income homes were observed in a summer day camp program, more than three-quarters of the children who had been rated as securely attached to their mothers as infants made friends easily, as compared to less than half of the campers who had been rated as insecurely attached in infancy (Elicker, Englund, & Sroufe 1992).

• Research reveals that early life insecure attachment patterns play out during the college dating years as a variety of clingy, overly jealous, or love-them-and-leave-them, interactions with romantic partners (Hazan & Shaver 1987).

• In intergenerational research, parents who lacked intimate loving as young children were found more likely to have babies rated as insecurely attached. The research tool most often used to identify adult patterns is the Adult Attachment Interview (AAI)[2] (Main & Goldwyn, in press).

• Grandmother AAI responses were related to attachment scores of grandbabies to their mothers. When 96 middle-class expectant mothers and their own mothers were interviewed, there was a significant concordance between grandmother and mother AAI classifications and a 68% match between pregnant mother AAI scores and their infants' attachment ratings at one year (Benoit & Parker 1994).

The intergenerational attachment data reveal the potential staying power of attachment patterns—secure and insecure—and their ability to influence later parenting styles. This increases the importance of providers being a positive force for ensuring all babies and children in their care a successful experience of trust in their caregiving.

When you nurture secure attachment in young children, you help them become more reflective and less likely to see the world in rigid terms of bad or good. Secure people are less likely to demand ideal behaviors from others. They are more likely to understand the complexities and human foibles of people they meet throughout life. They are less likely to be defensive and more likely to face negative emotional episodes with honesty, attempting to move on and enhance their lives rather than getting stuck in ruts of remembering and reacting negatively to difficult times in their past.

As you validate each child's essential goodness over and over during daily interactions, tuning in to their unique needs, you give the children in your care the priceless gift of secure attachment. This gift translates into more child courage, more competence, more friendliness, and the ability to rebound from life's troubles and empathize and cooperate with peers and adults—qualities every child care provider is eager for young children to achieve!

As a teacher, you are in the vanguard in ensuring that each child has a chance to develop a secure attachment with a caring adult in the classroom!

Chapter 1

Understanding Attachment

Sitting on the beach close to his mother and baby sister, 3-year-old Aaron digs in the sand with his shovel. He looks up and sees what appears to be a huge metal monster rolling toward them. Although the path to safety lies toward the board-walk, Aaron drops his shovel and leaps into his mama's lap, burying his face in her shoulder. His deep, secure attachment to his mother makes her the preferred source of safety—even when reason tells him that to escape "the monster" he should run away. Patting him soothingly, Aaron's mother explains that the machine is cleaning the beach and will certainly swerve around them, which in fact it does.

Child care providers and early childhood teachers hear a lot about attachment and how important it is for the emotional well-being of infants, toddlers, and preschoolers. But what exactly do we mean by attachment? What is meant when we say that Aaron is securely attached to his mother?

What is attachment?

The term *attachment* describes a strong emotional bond between a baby or young child and a caring adult who is part of the child's everyday life—the child's attachment figure. It is usually an affectionate or loving bond: the attachment of a child to his mother comes immediately to mind. However, a baby is not born with this attachment to his mother; it develops over time. Each day as the mother looks into the baby's eyes while nursing him; as she carries him in a pack on her chest, talking to him while raking leaves; or as she holds him on her lap, including him while reading to an older sibling, the baby's attachment to his mother grows stronger.

But what happens if the caring adult is not the baby's mother? Can someone besides the mother become an attachment figure? What if the father or an aunt cares for the baby each day while her mother is away at work? What happens if the baby is cared for in a center or family child care home by

---

Touch Is Special, Touch Is Crucial

Loving touch is a secret ingredient that magically helps babies and young children feel emotionally secure. Offer caresses, back rubs, and lap time freely. Make massages part of the daily routine for very young infants, and accompany your massages with quiet, soothing music (*Baby Massage* 1989). When diapering, you can kiss fingers and toes and tummy. Babies will grin and stretch their fingers toward you, "feeding" them to you for extra nibbly kisses.

Some children may be large or clumsy for their age. Some children may whine a lot; some may be rough or quick to show anger. Other children are wary and shy away from adult hugs or touches. Yet each child needs your loving touch—including those who shy away.

Some touch-shy children may have been abused or handled in ways that made them feel bad; other infants and toddlers are simply hypersensitive to touch. For children who seem to avoid adult touches, try an indirect approach: provide lap time or snuggle time. Be sure to rub the child's back at rest time. Sit next to the child and stroke his hair while you are talking to or reading with a small group.

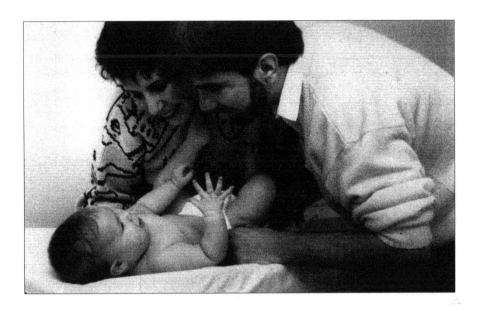

an adult who is not even related to her? Such situations are not at all unusual; many mothers work even when their babies are quite young. In these cases the baby will most likely become attached to the other adult—in addition to being attached to mom and dad. The bond between a baby and her parent tends to be a strong one, but babies and young children are capable of forming attachments to more than one adult. When a provider showers the babies and toddlers in her care with warmth, caring, and individual attention, those children are very likely to develop a secure bond with her (see "Touch Is Special, Touch Is Crucial"). Furthermore, children benefit from positive attachments to adults who are not their parents (Main & Weston 1981).

Attachment is a developmental system that builds slowly from a child's first days through his or her early years. It describes and explains people's enduring patterns of relationships from birth to death. From the infant's experiences and interactions during the first year with the key adult caregivers in her life—her attachment figures—she gradually builds up pictures of relationships between herself and others (Bowlby [1973] 2000). For the most part these internalized working models are not a part of the child's conscious thought, yet they have profound effects throughout life. The influence of these models plays a crucial role in the development of later personality. They are templates that serve as guides for and interpreters of emotions, perceptions, and behaviors in all future relationships (Bretherton & Waters 1985; Belsky & Nezworski 1988; Brazelton & Cramer 1990; Bretherton 1991; Crowell & Waters 1994; Colin 1996; De Wolff & van IJzendoorn 1997; Koops, Hoeksma, & van den Boom 1997).

Another key realm influenced by attachment is self-regulation. Children's ability to regulate their emotions and behaviors depends on the security of their attachments to caregivers and the quality of care they receive (Shore 1997). A child who is upset shows self-regulation when she soothes herself and re-

---

Is This Child Attached to Me?

How do you know when a baby or toddler is securely attached to you? If a baby cries when you leave the room, does that mean she has developed a strong bond with you? Probably, but no single behavior is a measurement of attachment (Moore et al. 1996). Crying upon separation is only one of a number of behaviors that point to secure attachment.

An infant or young child who is securely attached to you may call out to get your attention or reach out her arms to be picked up. A stressed baby or toddler may climb up onto your lap, cling to your leg, or suck on your knuckles to regain emotional equilibrium or bolster his courage before heading out again to explore his environment (Honig 1982). A toddler may interrupt her play to seek your attention, approach you, or just try to catch your eye, needing to know that you are nearby and available if she needs you. Your quick, warm response—an admiring glance, a warm hug, encouraging words, a gentle touch—reassures her while strengthening her attachment to you.

A baby who has securely bonded with you will smile in your direction and may follow you around. If he becomes apprehensive, he'll look to you for safety and encouragement. When distressed, he'll turn to you for comfort. This behavior is known as differential referencing. You are the child's safe base, his beacon of security. When you pick him up and soothe him with a hug, he will relax in your arms and mold comfortably to your body. Then he is ready to set out again to play, to learn more about his world, to interact with his peers, confident that his special person is watching out for him.

Secure Relationships

stores balance. For example, a baby in slight distress may calm herself by putting her fist in her mouth and sucking vigorously. Securely attached babies are more able to maintain physical and emotional balance than are insecurely attached babies (Matas, Arend, & Sroufe 1978; Sroufe 1979; Braungart-Reiker et al. 2001). Secure attachments also seem to prepare children to be confident and indepen-

dent learners with strong social skills (Ainsworth & Bell 1974; Arend, Gove, & Sroufe 1979; Erickson, Korfmacher, & Egeland 1992).[1]

The strength of attachment is such that the treatment and acceptance we grow up expecting from others corresponds to what we got from our own attachment figures. We tend to go through life feeling the way our attachment persons made us feel—be that happy or depressed, loved or neglected, at peace or in turmoil. The prospects are good that Aaron's loving, trusting relationship with his mother will predispose him to expect warm, healthy relationships with others in his childhood and throughout his life. Contrast Aaron's predisposition with that of a neglected or abused toddler. Based on her early experiences, she will likely expect cold, erratic relationships and little comfort in times of stress. These expectations may lead her to act in inappropriate ways in child care, such as showing anger or aggression toward an upset peer or not responding to warm adult overtures. Her difficult behaviors may ensnare an unwary caregiver and create a relationship fraught with punitive, unhappy interactions—like those the child has already come to expect. In the all-too-usual course of events, unhappiness and disappointment beget more unhappiness and disappointment.

Knowledge about attachment helps teachers, parents, and caregivers to understand how children's emotional behavioral styles and interactions are shaped and how the quality of early relationships affects later patterns of intimate relationships. This knowledge enables adults to temper their interactions to children's needs, thus influencing children's emotional security. Building secure attachment is a prime goal in early care and education; it is in fact the keystone for ensuring children's sound mental health (Honig 1993).

How does attachment work?

In the development of the attachment bond, a set of innate behaviors work together to help the infant gain a feeling of security through physical and emotional closeness to the mother or other caregiver. These are called *attachment behaviors,* although they are actually precursors to attachment—they are behaviors that foster attachment (Ainsworth 1973). The biological, or ethological, purpose of this behavioral system is to keep the infant close to the mother, who keeps the child out of harm's way:

Secure Relationships

Reassuring Songs

Create songs that show empathy for children's feelings, particularly if they are upset or very tired. In the morning, when a child is distressed about separating from her parents, use a well-known tune and repeat the child's name frequently as you invent a personal song that comforts and reassures her.

Use chants and melodies to ease transition times, so that children more readily cooperate, comply with classroom rules, or move to another activity. Sing the upbeat song "When You're Happy and You Know It" to lift children's energy levels (Crary & Steelsmith 1996). Use slow, quiet music to help babies and young children settle more easily into naptime.

Cradle songs—loving, tender, and soft—are perfect for soothing infants. Even if your first language is different from those of the infants and toddlers you care for, don't hesitate to sing the folk songs and lullabies of your home country at naptime. The warmth of your soft, melodic crooning will resonate with children of other backgrounds.

Countless old songs from different lands reflect the universality of this special genre. Some cradle songs are particularly beautiful in their tenderness of imagery—for example, the centuries-old Ladino lullaby, *"Durme, Durme, Hermozo Hijico"* (Sleep, Sleep, My Beautiful Little Son) (Commins 1967). African American cradle songs are among the most poignant. "All the Pretty Little Horses" lulls babies to sleep with promises: "Hush-a-bye, don't you cry; go to sleep little baby. / When you wake you shall have all the pretty little horses" (Honig 1995, 72). Babies respond to cradle songs from all times and in all languages.

Ethological theory [theory derived from the study of animal behavior] suggests that to ensure survival, nature has equipped babies with the ability to cry loud, cling to the caregiver, call, smile dazzlingly, lift arms to be picked up, creep, and follow a departing adult. With these fundamental postures and vocalizations, babies enhance their chances of survival through entraining their caregiver into a more caring, close relationship. (Honig 1993, 71)

Attachment, then, provides the child with a sense of security through a bond with a close, responsive adult. The baby gradually develops a level of confidence in the availability of his attachment figure or figures and how he may expect them to respond.

When an infant or toddler needs his mother or father and the parent responds readily and warmly, as in Aaron's case, secure attachment grows. When the adult is unavailable, the infant becomes agitated and distracted. He may signal his distress by calling out or crying. When the parent or caregiver heeds these signs of need—these attachment behaviors—the attachment bond is reinforced. On the other hand, if his signals fail to attract the adult, the infant becomes sad or depressed. Should the caregiver's unavailability and separation become a recurring pattern, the baby eventually develops unconscious defenses against stressful feelings of unhappiness and insecurity. The baby's defensive behaviors may show up as ignoring or avoiding the parent when she or he returns—signs of insecure attachment.

"Am I lovable?"

In addition to the baby's perceptions of the caregiver's availability and nurturance, especially in times of need or stress, at-

tachment has a second dimension: how the child perceives his own worthiness and lovability. A baby who has been neglected or abused may grow into a child who deems himself unlovable or a child victim who acts fearful in many situations. Or as described earlier, the child may behave in ways that exasperate and stress a teacher or caregiver to the point of responding sharply or showing strong disapproval. Without realizing it, this child has arranged the circumstances to confirm that he is unworthy of being loved.

Use Affirming Words that Encourage Children

Your encouraging words are like a magic tonic to a young child—they promote her confidence during exploratory play; they galvanize her motivation to persist at difficult learning tasks. Even before children understand words, they tune in to a positive, encouraging tone of voice. Adults' discouraging voice tones and harsh, scolding words are like ice cubes to children's souls. Children become fearful of venturing out on their own or exploring objects and situations; they are afraid of adult disapproval if they fail. Children wilt when they feel uncherished. Some children, as they grow older, become defiant and create mischief to get back at adults who so often seemed critical and unaccepting of them.

Adults' expressions of warmth and approval are spiritual or emotional vitamins. Children grow emotionally healthier if we affirm their small steps toward our goals for them rather than remind them of our worries about how far they are from meeting those goals. You have no doubt noticed that all children, whether they are typical or atypical in achieving developmental milestones, form a loving attachment to you if you nurture and admire them as they work toward new learning and understandings.

Juan is having a rough time adjusting to first grade. He has difficulty sitting in his seat for any length of time and is not learning the alphabet as quickly as the other children. If his teacher chastises him for sloppy work or troublesome behaviors, he usually cries. One day the teacher calls out, "Juan, stop crying. Children, let's vote: Who thinks Juan is a crybaby?" A number of children raise their hands. Juan looks down at the floor. His tears just fall harder.

If the caregiving environment does not improve for a young child like Juan, then his internal working models—his bad feelings about himself and low expectations for others' responses to him—are reinforced again and again by negative experiences. These internal representations may become quite difficult—although not impossible—to change without therapeutic help. If negative inner models persist, the children who hold them are likely in adulthood to become rejecting and unloving parents or even, in the extreme, fearsome abusers.

Thus a key feature of attachment is the child's notion of how acceptable or unacceptable he considers himself to be in the eyes of his attachment figures (Bowlby 1958). When attachment develops from healthy, positive relationships, the child has expectations of comfort and security and the sense of being worthy of such comfort and security. This is how John Bowlby, the founder of attachment theory, describes the process:

> When an individual is confident that an attachment figure will be available to him whenever he desires it, he will be much less prone to either intense or chronic fear than will an individual who for any reason has no such confidence. . . . Confidence in the availability of attachment figures, or a lack of it, is built up slowly during the years of immaturity . . . and whatever expectations are developed during those years tend to persist relatively unchanged throughout the rest of life. (1973, 235)

Strong as the internal models for attachment are, they are still subject to change in new or different circumstances. Toddlers' and preschoolers' growing abilities to integrate memories of experiences, thoughts, and feelings contribute to building their attachment representations. Being working models, these representations can evolve in different directions (Zeanah & Zeanah 1989). For children who have experienced attachment disturbances early in life—loss of a parent, abuse or neglect, or parents' divorce—or even for children whose parents are detached or disapproving, caregivers'

and teachers' perceptive insights, skills, and generous nurturance can make a positive difference. These sensitive, caring, attentive adults provide another opportunity for young children to form a secure attachment and reap some of the benefits such relationships offer.

Modern attachment theory

Our present understanding of attachment began with the work of Bowlby ([1969] 2000, [1973] 2000, [1980] 2000), the British child psychiatrist. Observing young children (between the ages of 1 and 4) in post-World War II hospitals and institutions who had been separated from their families, Bowlby concluded that to grow up mentally healthy, "the infant and young child should experience a warm and continuous relationship with his mother (or permanent mother substitute) in which both find satisfaction and enjoyment" (Bowlby [1969] 2000, 13).[2]

Bowlby's first formal statement of attachment theory, drawing heavily on ethological concepts, was presented in London in three now-classic papers read to the British Psychoanalytic Society. In the first, "The Nature of the Child's Tie to His Mother," presented in 1957, Bowlby (1958) proposed that a baby's attachment behaviors are innate and that they mature at various times during the beginning years. The behaviors include crying, smiling, following, and clinging. As the child develops, the behaviors begin to be activated by and linked to the mother figure. Bowlby's second and third papers, both presented in 1959, discuss his theories on separation anxiety and on grief and mourning in infancy and early childhood.

Bowlby's papers on attachment raised a storm of reaction from members of the Psychoanalytic Society. According to Freudian theory, the prevailing system at the time, an infant becomes attached to his mother because she satisfies his oral needs (Bemporad 1984). Bowlby veered from strict Freudian beliefs, concentrating on the importance of maternal attitude—warmth and emotional responsiveness—and the difficulties for the infant when separated from the mother.

Intrigued by Bowlby's theory, some researchers began investigating individual differences in infants' attachment behaviors toward their mothers as a secure base (Cassidy & Shaver 1999; Solomon & George 1999). Chief among these researchers was Mary Ainsworth. Having previously worked with Bowlby in London, Ainsworth (1967) began observing and interviewing Ugandan mothers with their infants. Her research led her to conclude that children can be either securely attached or insecurely attached. Further, she found that there were two main types of insecure attachments—ambivalent and avoidant (see "Kinds of Attachment").

Bowlby and Ainsworth met to discuss their research and common findings, and they laid out the principles that define modern attachment theory. They agreed that securely attached babies use their attachment figures as safe bases and react to them in positive ways. Babies recognize that their mothers or other caregivers are there to support them, and they gain strength from this knowledge. From the safe base of the attachment figure, babies

Kinds of Attachment

By analyzing infants' reunion behaviors with the mother using the Strange Situation technique at ages 12 months and 18 months (see endnote 3), researchers note different kinds of attachment patterns. **Securely attached** babies actively seek reunion; they sink into and mold onto the body of their primary caregiver. Having "touched base" and relaxed deeply, these babies are ready to leave the security of the mother's lap to go back to their play with the toys.

Babies who begin to seek comfort from the mother or other primary caregiver during the Strange Situation, but then turn away in anger or irritability or struggle to get down from the caregiver's arms, are identified as **ambivalent/insecure** babies. When a baby shows this kind of response, the parent has likely been insensitive to the baby's tempos, rhythms, and distress signals in her relationship with the infant. For example, the parent may pick up or attend to the infant at her own convenience or whim rather than when the baby expresses a need.

Some babies do not seek the parent upon her reentry. They ignore the adult and continue to play with toys. These are **avoidant/insecure** babies. While they look as if they are "mature" in accepting separations, they often turn out to be angry at home and hostile and unfeeling with preschool peers (Honig 1993, 71). Belsky (1988) explains that for babies with avoidant/insecure attachments, anger and lack of trust in the attachment figure increase the child's later risk for social difficulties, lack of compliance, lack of cooperation, and increased aggressiveness or bullying of other children.

More recently, Mary Main has built on Ainsworth's work, identifying a third type of insecure attachment, which she calls dazed or disoriented (Hesse & Main 2000). Babies characterized as **disoriented/insecure** seem disorganized or even dazed, lacking purposeful goals. In the Strange Situation they display contradictory behavior patterns, such as moving toward their mother for reunion, then interrupting the movement, looking confused, and not continuing toward the goal of proximity or comfort (Main & Weston 1981). Or they may strongly avoid the parent on reunion and then strongly seek closeness. They may appear tentative, suddenly halting their movement toward the attachment figure as if confused, apprehensive, or depressed (Main & Solomon 1990).

explore the environment. Infants express their feelings and communicate even negative feelings openly with the mother or other caregiver. They trust that this adult will be accessible and responsive if they need comfort, reassurance, care, or attention. Whereas secure babies tend to cry very little when their mothers leave, insecure babies seem to cry quite a lot, even when their mothers are with them. Nonattached babies do not seem to care whether or not their mothers are present; they have frequently been left alone for long periods of time and have not formed strong attachments.

Ainsworth assessed the security of children's attachments using a technique of her own known as the Strange Situation.[3] This technique involves observing at 12 months and again 18 months how an infant reacts to her mother and to a stranger during periods of separation and reunion. The procedure may be used to measure an infant's relationship with any person—not just the mother—who may serve as an attachment figure for the baby.

All mothers are not the same

Ainsworth and her colleagues (Ainsworth, Bell, & Stayton 1971; Stayton, Hogan, & Ainsworth 1971) found that infants' attachment styles seem to correspond to sets of parental behaviors. Mothers of secure infants are sensitive and responsive; they

• hold the baby in a tenderly careful way

- enjoy close cuddles and playful, affectionate interactions with the baby

- feed in tempo with infant needs and feeding styles

- give babies floor freedom to play

- interpret infant emotional signals sensitively

- respond promptly and appropriately to infant distress

- provide contingent feedback (respond immediately and purposefully to infant behaviors they want to reinforce or discourage) in face-to-face interactions during routines and play

In contrast, mothers of insecurely attached infants tend to be inconsistent, unpredictable, and intrusive (Belsky, Rovine, & Taylor 1984). Specifically, mothers of babies categorized as being ambivalently attached tend to pick up, hold, kiss, and cuddle their babies when it suits them, without regard to the babies' needs or activities. These mothers may be self-absorbed, making them inconsistent in care rather than responsively attuned to the baby's signs of distress or need. They act on their own wishes and needs above all and may be intrusive and overcontrolling. In a play situation with the infant, they try to dominate rather than follow the child's signals (Greenspan 1990).

Mothers of babies with avoidant/insecure attachments show a different pattern. They seem to dislike close bodily contact with the baby. They tend to be rigid and unexpressive ners, then those infants are as likely as other infants to be securely attached to the mother at 1 year. Furthermore, therapeutic interventions can be effective.

In research conducted in Holland with families with highly irritable first-born babies (van den Boom 1994, 1997), home visitors worked with half of the infant-mother pairs every three weeks, teaching the mothers individually how to interpret their babies' unique cues and respond effectively. The home visitors showed these mothers how to become accurate observers of their babies' signals. For example, they encouraged them to imitate some baby behaviors, such as vocalizations, and respect others, such as the infant avoiding eye contact. They promoted playful mother-child interactions with toys and highlighted the importance of soothing the crying infant, individualizing techniques for each mother.

How effective was the program? At the end of a year infants in the intervention group were more sociable, better able to soothe themselves, and engaged in cognitively more sophisticated exploration than the babies in the control group. And significantly more intervention babies (62%) than control babies (28%) were classified as securely attached to their mothers.

Where secure attachment is concerned, temperament is not destiny. The more that parents and other caregivers learn to tune in visually and respond appropriately to infant cues, the less the risk of attachment disorders for irritable infants.

emotionally with their babies. They also seem more resentful, irritable, and angry than do others. More rejecting than other mothers, they are likely to express less positive emotions. Bus and colleagues (1997) recorded this fragment of a five-minute book-reading session between an avoidant/insecure baby and the mother, who could not evoke the child's interest in a book:

Mother: *(turns the page while the child is looking around in the room and reads)* The Book of Babies.

Child: *(tries to leave the mother's lap by pushing at the mother's arm)*

Mother: Look, look, look. *(turns the page)*

Mother: Ah, look at this.

Child: *(the child tries to escape under the book)*

Mother: *(reads the literal text)* Making faces, kicking, crawling, busy hands . . .

Child: *(standing on the floor and walking around)*

Mother: You don't wanna read, do you? Come here. *(with an angry voice)* (Bus et al. 1997, 93)

In reading the picture book, this mother did not change her tone of voice or style of reading to capture the baby's interest in a shared reading experience (Honig & Brophy 1996). Nor did the mother attempt to modify the text to help the baby focus on the pictures and the story; instead, she accused the baby of lacking interest in the book.

Mothers of infants characterized as dazed or disoriented in regard to attachment have typically had their own attachment-related traumas as children (Hesse & Main 2000). Often these mothers are severely depressed or otherwise mentally ill; they may also be drug dependent. The distant and inappropriate behaviors these mothers show toward their children lead to this severest form of insecure attachment.

Home sweet home base

Attachment is the first social-behavioral system to develop, as babies with their need for attention and reassurance interact with one or more caregivers. As the attachment system evolves, it interacts with two other emerging systems: exploration/curiosity and fear/wariness arousal.

A fearful or worried baby is less likely to explore adventurously. A well-cuddled baby with an available and intimately tuned-in caregiver is more likely to feel secure enough to toddle off on splendid adventures, knowing that the special attachment figure is there for her. Indeed, a well-fed, well-rested baby often crawls off on all fours to explore toys in a playroom without a glance back at the secure attachment figure. For this baby, the caregiver remains a touchstone for security, comfort, and protection in case of stress, fatigue, or perceived danger.

A tired baby or a discouraged toddler may well need to crawl or gallop back and throw himself onto the caregiver. A worried baby needs the security of the caregiver's shoulder. Reassuring arms and a welcoming, familiar lap create a deeply satisfying refueling station for a young child.

> *Tanya is building an awesomely high tower of cardboard blocks—even taller than her toddler self. Another toddler, cheerfully and heedlessly hurrying past, brushes by the carefully built tower, and down it falls. Tanya turns away in aggravation and disappointment, throwing herself onto the welcoming lap of her caregiver Jim, who is stretched out on the floor watching several toddlers at play.*

We know that babies or toddlers have formed attachments when they cry, call, or reach out like Tanya to the special adult. When tired or frightened or uneasy, they may cling to that person, and if they are mobile they often crawl or toddle after her or him. As we have seen, they show greater freedom in exploring the environment when they have their secure base, the attachment figure, close at hand. In a variety of ways babies and toddlers show particular responsiveness to those special persons to whom they are attached:

> *Although 9-month-old Jared has been assigned to Delores's special care for three months, his face rarely brightens and he does not respond with vocalizations when Delores coos to him and talks to him as she diapers or carries him around. "I'm worried about Jared," Delores confides to her supervisor. The supervisor quietly reassures her, saying, "Keep the faith, Delores. You are cuddling, talking, personally cherishing this baby. It may take a while before he feels confident enough to trust." A few weeks later Delores bubbles with good news: Jared burst into tears when she left on coffee break!*

Why is Delores thrilled that Jared burst into tears? For one simple reason: he is showing his attachment to her.

When Delores returned to the room, she was delighted to see Jared reach out his arms to her to be picked up. Now he actively participates in all the interpersonal games she has been patiently trying for months—pat-a-cake, peekaboo, and imitations of "bababa" and "mamama."

Summary

During the first years of a child's life, attachment is an active, growing, behavioral system that develops with respect to specific caregiving persons the baby trusts to provide safety, comfort, and reassurance. Security of attachment depends on the caregivers' abilities to sensitively and reliably help the baby "maintain organized behavior in the face of increasingly high levels of arousal" (Sroufe 1979, 837). When babies feel secure, safe, and deeply sure that their special persons are there for

Secure Relationships

them, they move out to explore with vigor, absorbed in play. If they become alarmed or feel abandoned or threatened, their attachment needs surge. Then they—like Aaron—seek proximity to their beacons of safety, their attachment figures, who know so well how to cope and provide the reassurance and soothing they need.

An individual's early experiences and interactions with his special adults create patterns of behavior and expectations for others' behavior toward him (Karen 1994). These internal models influence a child's interactions with others—peers, teachers, other adults—throughout childhood; they shape the child's personality.

Clearly, attachment must be a priority and concern for all those caring for young children. Intimate attachments to others are the hub around which a person's life revolves, not only as an infant or a toddler but throughout adolescence and the years of maturity and into old age (Bowlby [1980] 2000). Secure attachment also influences a baby's predisposition to explore her universe. For babies and toddlers whose homes do not provide the love, comfort, and attention necessary for secure attachment, the nurturing support of a skilled and caring provider or teacher can make all the difference.

Chapter 2

Attachment to Early Childhood Caregivers

Two weeks before returning to work, Jeannine visits several child care centers to enroll 4-week-old Marcus, but is unable to find one with space for an infant. Following the recommendation of a neighbor, Jeannine counts herself lucky to find Mrs. Philips, a family child care provider who lives nearby. Mrs. Philips is kind and attentive to Marcus, and he seems to thrive in her care.

Unfortunately, after only two months, Mrs. Philips is called out of town to help her daughter, who is experiencing child care problems of her own. Jeannine makes temporary arrangements to leave Marcus with a friend until she finds a new provider. She and her husband notice that Marcus is somewhat fussy in the evenings, and he cries in the mornings when they leave him with their friend. They wonder if they are spoiling him.

Finally Jeannine finds another caregiver who comes highly recommended, Ms. Tilden. But when Jeannine drops off Marcus at Ms. Tilden's, he has a temper tantrum. Embarrassed, Jeannine leaves quickly, hoping that Marcus will do better when she is out of sight. Although he eventually quiets down, Marcus is nearly inconsolable later upon waking from his nap, despite Ms. Tilden's warm attempts to comfort him.

What's going on here? Is Marcus spoiled, as his parents suspect? Should Jeannine be embarrassed because her infant son is upset when she leaves? The obvious answer to both questions is no. What has happened is that all of the uprooting in Marcus's young life has interrupted the attachment process.

Stable relationships with the same loving adults allow secure attachments to develop, but Marcus has experienced one change after another. First, Marcus left the security of his home after only six weeks. Then, just as Marcus was getting used to Mrs. Philips, he was removed from her care—another disruption of a building relationship. Until he is able to form a bond with Ms. Tilden, his life—and sense of security—will be in flux.

Like Marcus, all babies need the security of knowing that their needs will be consistently met by familiar loved ones. When someone whom they trust to always be there for them—someone like Mrs. Philips—is suddenly removed from their world, babies' sense of well-being evaporates.

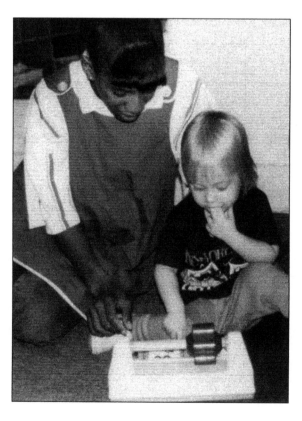

Babies need continuity of care

Attachment can be said to stem from two components. First, there is the quality of caregiving experiences. When caregivers respond to babies in the consistently nurturing and responsive ways described throughout this book, they promote attachment. Second, attachment depends on an ongoing relationship between child and adult. For secure attachment to occur, children need to have a sustained experience with a special caregiver.

I've Grown Accustomed to Your Face

Close reciprocal relationships do not happen overnight. It takes time for a caregiver to become familiar to a child. Adults need to provide infants with focused attention over a long period of time, looking into their eyes, cuddling them, and talking to them during dressing and feeding and diapering intervals.

By having just a few babies in her care, the caregiver comes to know them well and learns how best to respond to each child's temperament, needs, and cues (Lally et al. 1991). Each baby and her special adult form their own pattern of communication as trust, intimacy, and confidence grow between them. Over time the caregiver gets to know the children's families as well, building partnerships with them.

Thus, it is vital for every child in an early childhood program to have a primary caregiver with the major responsibility for her daily care. The loving, nurturing provider becomes a secure base for the child, who develops strong feelings of attachment as he basks in the warmth of his caregiver's admiring glances and tender hugs.

Young children are quite conservative about changes in their lives. They may show distress when faced with unfamiliar caregivers and peers in a new child care setting. Research has shown that continuity of care—keeping children with the same caregiver—tends to deepen children's confidence by ensuring that their special adult really knows them and is attuned to their needs (Raikes 1993). This practice allows the caregiver to learn her babies' tempos, personalities, needs, fears, styles of feeding, and comfortable positions for cuddling, reading, and soothing.

Because the need for secure attachment does not end with infancy, it is also desirable to ensure that the same high-quality caregiver stay with her babies not only throughout the infancy period, but ideally to 36 months (Essa et al. 1999). As a baby grows into toddlerhood, with its seesawing struggles of autonomy versus doubt/shame/rage (Erikson [1950] 1993), the need for a deep and basic sense of caregiver trustworthiness continues. Long, leisurely years of getting to know one another increase the chance for a baby to develop secure infant-caregiver attachment and for the caregiver to have strong bonds with the child.

How to nurture attachment

While we know the importance of parental bonding, the importance of the baby's attachment to the out-of-home caregiver is not always as obvious. The caregiver who is aware of how crucial the gift of love is for very young children—and who acts on that knowledge by cherishing those in her care—increases the chances of each child forming a secure attachment to her. For the baby who already has a strong bond with a family member, intimacy and trust with the provider is a bonus. For the infant or child without a secure attachment at home, a warm, nurturing relationship with the provider is crucial. It opens the door to the many positive influences stemming from secure attachment—feelings of being lovable, validation of the child's self-worth, a model for positive interactions—a door that might otherwise remain shut. For this baby, secure attachment to the provider is a godsend.

Here are some important things for caregivers to keep in mind in fostering young children's attachment.

Beginning with love

The first ingredient in attachment is love. The idea that paid caregivers "love" the children in their care may make some uncomfortable. Yet no one would dispute the idea that caregivers must have warm, nurturing feelings toward the babies in their care. Call it what we will, its essence is love.

Some co-workers or parents may misinterpret a caregiver's loving interactions as unprofessional. They may feel that child care is a business meant to provide a safe and stimulating environment, but not one in which providers should be emotionally involved with children in their care. However, this is a misconception. A special bond between caregiver and child is important for the child's emotional well-being and development.

Infants become more and more secure in their special relationships with caregivers who nourish and protect them and are available on a regular, predictable basis. When a working parent can nurture the development of this intimate emotional relationship only part of the time, and an infant is in group care, then it is crucial in the care setting that one or two familiar people be available to the child over time (Honig 1985a). As Baker and

Manfredi-Petitt concluded from their in-depth interviews with family child care workers, "Despite social taboos, it is left to caregivers to bridge the gap left by working parents and ensure that children, especially infants and toddlers, are encircled with love" (1998, 7).

Treating babies and young children with respect

A second requirement for building secure attachment is respect. How do providers show respect to babies and young children? They treat each child as a special, well-loved person; show them small courtesies, such as using their names frequently; speak in a calm tone of voice rather than an overcontrolling one; behave respectfully even with children whose actions pose challenges or are puzzling (Honig 1989).

When caregivers leave the room to get supplies or go on a break, they should never depart abruptly. The provider may want to adopt the habit of saying in words, even to an infant, where she's going and that she will be back soon. Although babies and toddlers do not fully understand what the adult is saying, she conveys concern and respect for their feelings. Older toddlers, as they begin to pick up on meaning and tone, are reassured to know that the caregiver will be back. Because babies and young children count on the caregiver's availability for nurturance, she needs to let them know about her goings and comings—especially about her coming back.

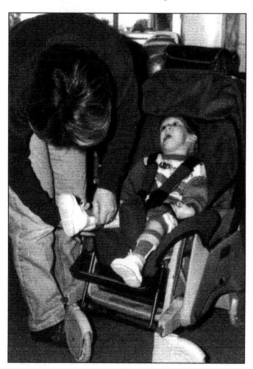

Supporting young children's efforts

Babies and toddlers need the kind of warm, unobtrusive attention that helps them build confidence in their special adults' caring and promotes positive social

Practice Positive Guidance

Adopt a wide variety of appropriate guidance techniques. Your goal is to nurture self-control and empathy in young children while building secure, mutually satisfying relationships with each of them. Help children find win-win solutions to their conflicts.

Here are some ideas to more effectively assist young children to become ego-resilient, self-disciplined people.

• Catch children being good and express pleasure at appropriate behaviors.

• Model considerateness, patience, courtesy, and helpfulness.

• Admire the efforts and attempts of a less skilled child.

• Use hugs, shining eyes, and a loving voice tone to build children's basic trust in adults as helpful people whose expressions of approval are important and pleasurable.

• Hold a child on your lap in front of a mirror and initiate games of facial and body imitations to establish an awareness of body boundaries and self-image.

• Say what you *do* want when possible, rather than what you *don't* want. "Please walk slowly!" is easier to carry out than "Please don't run!"

• Physically hold a child who is out of control. Tell her or him, "I know you are feeling very upset. I will help you calm down so that you don't get hurt or hurt someone else. I'll help you be safe until you can get back in control."

A rich repertoire of positive guidance approaches belongs in every teacher's emotional first-aid kit.

Adapted, with permission, from A.S. Honig, "Research in Review: Compliance, Control, and Discipline—Part 2." *Young Children* 40 (March 1985): 50–51.
Note: For a brief list of resources for positive guidance techniques, see endnote 1 for this chapter.

exchanges. This is a subtle balance between laissez-faire approaches that let children "do their own thing" without the caregiver's help, and intrusive, discouraging techniques that make a child feel she cannot succeed on her own.

Bobby plays with a wooden train set on the floor. His mom is nearby. Every time the toddler tries to add a new car to the train or tries to couple two cars, his mother snatches them away and berates him: "That's not the way they go. Here, I'll do it. This is the way the cars are supposed to hook together. You're doing it wrong." After a number of intrusive interruptions, Bobby sweeps away the trains in a heap.

Finding that "just right" voice tone, that helpful assist, those thoughtful words that encourage and focus a child on the problem without taking away his initiative is important. Such achievements pose an exhilarating professional challenge for teachers of very young children, and they really make a difference.

When a teacher becomes skilled at finding this middle road in supporting a child's efforts, not only does she increase the child's chances to form a secure attachment to her, but she also helps advance mental development. Vygotsky talks about the *zone of proximal development* in which the adult is able to help children progress from their present level of independent problem solving to a higher developmental level "through problem solving under adult guidance" ([1930–1935] 1978, 86).

Keeping it light

Humor, while not a prerequisite, is certainly a boon to attachment. Young children—like all of us—find life's difficulties easier to take when approached with a sense of humor. When disagreement or contention with a child occurs, a

Attachment and Cognitive Development

Child development experts have often chosen to study *either* children's socio-emotional development *or* their intellectual development, as if these two very important aspects of a child were entirely separate. Yet loving and learning are deeply intertwined.

Secure attachments seem to prepare children to be confident and independent learners with strong social skills (Ainsworth & Bell 1974; Erickson, Korfmacher, & Egeland 1992). Particularly of interest is how early emotional trust and security are related to the ways in which young children learn to learn—the ways in which they tackle difficult puzzles in preschool or learn to pay attention to the teacher in elementary school.

Children with severe disorders of attachment often have learning difficulties that baffle teachers. Researchers have shed light on these difficulties by studying how attachment affects aspects of attention and cognition. For example, attention span tends to be greater among children securely attached to their mothers (Easterbrooks & Goldberg 1990). Clinicians and researchers found that solving cognitive tasks is more successful for children when they feel loved and worthy of being loved (Matas, Arend, & Sroufe 1978).[2]

Secure Relationships

light touch, a smile, a wrinkled nose and grin, or silly rhyming words are sometimes an effective antidote. All of these can defuse what could otherwise become a tug of wills that decreases the chances for building a loving and intimate relationship with that young child (Honig 1988). Viewing an irksome situation from a humorous perspective can also lighten the load on caregivers.

It's the end of lunch and Esther has just finished washing up an infant in his high chair and is going on to clean the face and hands of another baby nearby. Glancing back at the first baby, Esther sees that she neglected to take away the bowl with the uneaten portion of his vegetable soup. The soup is now dribbling down the surprised baby's face from his hair, where he has just poured it. Esther's cleanup job is becoming a highly involved enterprise! Reframing the situation humorously, she reminds herself that a vegetable facial treatment would really be quite expensive in a beauty salon. The cleanup job now seems less onerous.

Strategies for strengthening attachment

In addition to being a stable, nurturing presence in children's lives, caregivers can use a number of specific strategies to facilitate the attachment process.

Embed Your Loving Interactions in Ordinary Daily Routines

The emotional curriculum to build secure attachment cannot be packaged in 10-minute periods of individual attention. Daily routines provide secret spaces and unscheduled moments for you to weave respect, trust, and empathy into your relationships with the young children in your care.

When you are involved in routines such as setting out food, washing up a child's messy hands, carrying a baby to the window to look at raindrops, or even wiping a drippy nose, engage in turn-taking talk. Such give-and-take affirms the importance of the child's communications, no matter how garbled her message may be. Use daily diapering and feeding times for intimate communication with babies and toddlers, who will babble away earnestly in response.

Creating a safe emotional climate

Erikson ([1950] 1993) maintained that the emotional climate within which an infant grows up affects the extent to which she becomes an active, curious, self-motivated learner who cooperates with caregivers and persists at challenging tasks. The caregiver's sensitive responsiveness to a baby's routine and individual needs creates a sense of trust that becomes the basis of the baby's early identity.

In the late 1960s and early 1970s the Family Development Research Program in Syracuse, New York, was one of the first early childhood programs to translate into practice Eriksonian theory and the work on attachment. To promote optimum mental health for very young children, every aspect of programming, and particularly routines connected to bodily necessities and comfort such as diapering, feeding, and soothing into naptime, became important opportunities to foster the growth of a secure bond between baby and caregiver. Four babies were assigned to each caregiver, and the caregivers were responsible for getting to know each infant intimately. Warm, caring practices like these, pioneered some 40 years ago, are now used more widely and are promoted by such groups as Zero to Three and NAEYC.

Responding to children's body language

Well-honed noticing skills are vital tools in promoting attachment. They serve to clue in a caregiver to the quiet child who needs a warm hug, personalized attention, or some intimate talk while playing together with an interesting toy. Small bodily cues from children can be an excellent indication of their emotions. These cues also help the caregiver figure out temperament styles that need to be addressed in special ways adapted to each child's needs (Honig 1992, 1993, 1997) (see "Attachment Difficulties or Temperament?" Chapter 1, p. 14).

For instance, a withdrawn, shy child who tends to look away when the caregiver tries to catch her eye may get less adult attention than the child who smiles back. Although some youngsters may not seek much attention, they still need their caregiver to check in with reassuring, loving looks. They too need quiet touches and "together times" that tell them how much their special adult cares for and enjoys them.

A caregiver can also tune in to signals of stress. If a baby is fussy or crabby, even when he has recently been fed and diapered, the provider takes note. Maybe the child needs to burp; maybe he

---

Notice with Your Ears and Eyes

Keep your antennae attuned to the unspoken messages of children's body language. Confirm for children that you notice how they feel and you hear and understand their reactions—even though you cannot allow them to retaliate if another child hits, for example, or snatches a toy.

The teacher ties one toddler's shoelaces and then gets ready to take another toddler for a diaper change. Isaac comes over with a book for his teacher to read to him. His brow furrows when he sees how busy she is with other children. "Isaac," says his teacher gently, "are you feeling angry? Did you want me to read your book right now? As soon as I get Lana clean, we will read your book together. Okay?" Isaac's eyes widen. How could his teacher read his mind so well!

Your focused attention, active listening, and caring response reassure a child that her special adult understands her anger, fears, feelings of resentment, and sometimes overwhelming emotions.

---

needs some crooning, wordless murmuring and a rhythmic pat-pat-pat on his body to help him settle soundly into sleep. If a baby is very tiny, he may need to be snuggled in a baby carrier on an adult's chest so that as the adult moves about, the baby can feel the rhythms, motion, and warmth of her body.

Sometimes a baby needs a ride around the room on the crook of an arm to visit interesting places such as a mirror, where she grins at her reflection. Perhaps a child needs to lean against the teacher as they settle down together for a cozy interval of picture book reading. Maybe a toddler is being pressured too much too soon for early toilet learning, and he needs a more flexible, easygoing approach to the potty.

A child's body language speaks volumes. Eyes that fail to sparkle often signal that a young child does not feel connected to a loving adult. Stiff shoulders and gritted teeth sometimes indicate that a young child feels he will need to fight or defend himself by hitting another child at the slightest perceived threat to his wellbeing. Grinding teeth at naptime, lashing out

at peers, excessive self-stimulation—these body signs are clues that the child is tense or unhappy. Teachers can create a mental health checklist as they watch children and read their body signals. Reading children's body language boosts a caregiver's ability to provide more individualized creature comforts for each of them (Honig 1986a, 1986b, 1993, 2000b).

Mental Health Checklist of Behaviors and Body Signals

Are the young children in your care thriving emotionally? Perceptive awareness and monitoring of baby and toddler behaviors is your first line of defense against emotional troubles. The following body cues, especially when you see several in the same child, indicate that the child's mental health may be in jeopardy.

❑ dull, unsparkling eyes

❑ back arching and body stiffening as a regular response

❑ avoidance of eye contact

❑ pushing away from rather than relaxed body molding to the caregiver

❑ limp, floppy, listless body

❑ rare smiles despite tender adult elicitation

❑ compulsive body rocking, thumb sucking, self-stimulation

❑ inconsolable crying for long periods

❑ scattered attention during intimate exchanges with caregiver

❑ apathetic facial expression

❑ lack of empathy—impassiveness or anger when a peer is hurt or distressed

❑ lack of responsiveness to warm adult overtures

❑ long and frequent temper tantrums

❑ fearful withdrawal or flinching from caregiver's caress

❑ anxious shadowing of or clinging to provider even after months in care

❑ regular avoidance of or indifference to parents at pickup time

❑ continuous biting or hitting of others without provocation

❑ little or no interest in peers or others

❑ grimaces of despair

❑ going too easily between adults with no sign that any one caregiver is special

❑ persistent head banging against crib

❑ tendency to run off, heedless of the caregiver's presence as a safe base

❑ aimless wandering; inability to focus or settle into constructive play

❑ reckless actions that endanger the child; lack of awareness of body limits

❑ overly anxious or overly compliant with adults

❑ oversolicitousness toward adults—parentification

If you observe a child showing clusters of the behaviors listed above, work with family members to alleviate the child's stress. In some cases you may need to help families connect with community resources to support the emotionally distressed baby.

Adapted, with permission, from A.S. Honig, "Mental Health for Babies: What Do Theory and Research Teach Us?" *Young Children* 48 (March 1993), 72.

Using books to help children deal with their feelings

Many books are designed to help children cope with loss, sadness, worry, fears, and anger. Look for books in which the children or animal characters have a difficult problem and the story shows how each character copes in order to solve the problem. Suzy Kline's *Don't Touch!* is a book toddlers ask teachers to read over and over. Because some children have heard those words so often, the story seems to strike a chord. Hearing how the child in the book works out his feelings about the grownups who yell at him seems to satisfy the spirit of many a child.

Choose books that allow children to identify with characters who are kind and helpful. The Dr. Seuss books about Horton the friendly and caring elephant are excellent choices.

For infants and toddlers other good choices include the Sam books, written by Barbro Lindgren. Sam is a toddler who often gets into a tussle over a cookie or a toy. Hearing how Sam's mama resolves the situation by providing the children with separate toys or treats helps toddlers understand that adults try

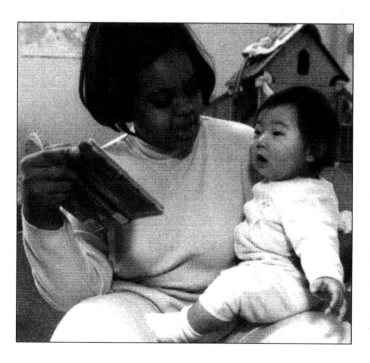

to be fair. A child can call on his special adults as a positive source for help in resolving social fusses and fights.

Books as bibliotherapy can help children gain the insight and courage to cope with difficult situations, such as divorcing parents, a mother who yells, life without a daddy, or jealousy toward a new sibling.

Introduce Babies and Toddlers to Books

Reading to young children boosts their language skills and begins a life-long love affair with books. Sit a baby or toddler on your lap while you read, so she can see and touch (and perhaps taste!) the sturdy oilcloth or laminated pages. Or encourage two or three children at a time to snuggle up close where they can lean against you while you read, pointing to the pictures and talking about the story. A small baby in a seat or on the floor will gaze at a propped-up book as you turn the pages and name and describe the familiar items pictured. Simple pictures of animals, clothing, foods, and faces hold an infant's attention.

It is important for parents to hear about how much their children enjoy reading books with you. Encourage parents to read to infants and toddlers at home. You may want to model for parents reading techniques with young children (Honig & Brophy 1996). Compile a book list with brief blurbs to hand out when parents ask you for book suggestions, and leave copies in a stack for parents to pick up. Families will appreciate ideas on books to promote peacefulness and feelings of being loved. *The Runaway Bunny* by Margaret Wise Brown, about a mother bunny's determination to seek out her beloved little bunny when he runs away, is a good choice. So is Clyde Watson's *Catch Me and Kiss Me and Say It Again*, which offers rhymes for dressing, bathing, feeding, and toe-tickling time with infants and toddlers. For helping toddlers settle down at sleep time, *Goodnight Moon*, also by Margaret Wise Brown, is a perennial favorite.

Teaching children group entry skills

Part of attachment involves a young child's relating comfortably to the other children in the room. The observant caregiver notices the child who finds it hard to connect with peers: a toddler hovering on the edge of a group of children playing together, not knowing how to say "Can I play too?" or a child who hasn't a clue about how to join another child in pulling a wagonful of blocks around the room.

Sometimes, however, the teacher noticing a yearning child may intercede in an intrusive manner, insisting that the others let the child play. Or she may urge the child to act without providing specific suggestions, saying, "Why don't you go and play with your friends?" Without specific adult assistance, some children may use inappropriate or inept behaviors, acting bossy or aggressive or grabby (Honig & Thompson 1994).

Some children may be welcomed by others to join their play but not know how to respond. Others may know how to enter into group play but lack the skills to extend or continue the play. When caregivers notice these situations, they can provide a priceless boost in understanding and skill for young children by scaffolding peer play or modeling the necessary social skills.

Creating a responsive environment

The creation of a responsive physical environment likewise promotes attachment. Caregivers can arrange the environment to promote a child's ease and comfort with being in child care. Soft pillows, mattresses with washable covers, areas carpeted with rugs—these are some of the furnishings, textures, and materials that lend a feeling of coziness and warmth to a child care facility or family child care home. Holding a child in a rocking chair (located where there is no chance of hurting little fingers or toes) is a good way to ease an infant's entry into a program or a preschooler's anxiety when upsetting feelings sweep over him. Caregivers can rock infants who need soothing pats or young children who need some quiet, intimate attention.

Fresh flowers in vases and plants with green trailing vines in hanging pots add richness to the world of the nursery. A colorful banner hung from the ceiling catches children's attention and may even prompt some preschoolers to imagine they are living in a castle in olden times!

Early childhood settings need a cozy reading nook safe from tumbling toddlers and the feet of galloping children. Locating the reading area in a corner helps children focus quietly on books, either alone or in the company of a friend or teacher.

A nurturing environment gives children the message that this is a place where a child with a picture book can stretch out on a special furry rug or sink into a comfy beanbag chair. A cubby with the inner walls covered in soft, textured fabric provides another spot for children to be alone and recharge their batteries. An overstimulated child can sit quietly and watch, regaining her equilibrium before rejoining the group.

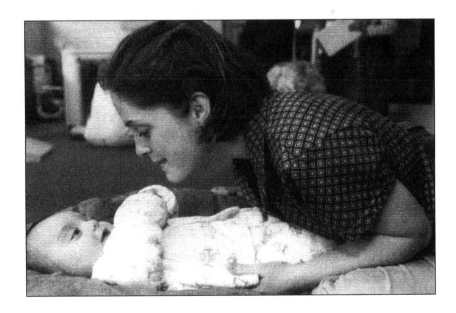

Conclusion

Attachment, that unique system built up between a child and each of his special caregiving individuals, is one of the most valuable gifts a child can receive. Babies need to have consistent high-quality care with the same provider—the longer, the better. Without continuity of warm, responsive care, children are less likely to become attached, secure, and confident individuals.

Caregivers are a precious resource. The sensitivity and caring they show every day and over time ensure that each child has the opportunity to develop a secure attachment and thus reap the long-term benefits that attachment offers.

Chapter 3

Parents, Caregivers, and Attachment

My "crazy about my kids" feelings were awakened the day I first became a father. When Linsey was born, her umbilical cord was unusually short, making the delivery long and difficult. When she emerged, her body was blue and her lungs severely congested.

Linsey was whisked away from her mother to the Intensive Care Unit, with a new and worried father in tow. She required several hours of intensive care (and intensive prayers) to get her to "pink up." I spent the earliest hours of Linsey's life holding her hand through an incubator, talking to her, comforting her. Given this experience, it's no wonder I quickly became very attached and protective of her. In fact, these feelings linger as this bright and lovely young lady approaches her 14th birthday.

—Steve Duncan, 1997
"Be Warm, Loving, and
Responsive to Your Children"

Here's a father who is deeply attached to his child from birth right into her teen years—how unusual. Or is it? In many cases it seems like including fathers in the event of their child's birth sets the stage for paternal participation throughout children's young lives. When the father develops a strong bond with the child, does that mean the mom takes a backseat? Not really. Children can be attached to dad as well as mom, and they usually are. But the nature of these relationships depends on how involved each parent is with the child and his routine care (Caldera, Huston, & O'Brien 1995; Belsky 1996; De Wolff & van IJzendoorn 1997).

Mothers and fathers

Most infants appear to develop a stronger attachment to the primary caregiver (Lamb 1997). And although fathers are very important emotional partners for young children, mothers are the primary caregivers and attachment figures in many families. In the majority of households mothers carry out a greater portion of routine daily baby care, such as diapering, feeding, bathing, and comforting the infant (Pitzer & Hessler 1992). Whatever their involvement in their children's care, fathers need to know that they do play a very significant role in the child's development, and they may need support in ways to fulfill this role (Lamb, Pleck, & Levine 1985; Lamb 1997).

Each Attachment Is Different

Attachment is relationship-specific, not infant-specific (Sroufe 1983; Fox, Kimmerly, & Schafer 1991; Steele, Steele, & Fonagy 1996). That is, a baby is able to build secure attachments with several persons— a parent, a child care provider or teacher, an admiring aunt, uncle, or grandparent. Yet each attachment is unique. The child responds to each caregiver's small daily gestures of care, and over time the child creates subconscious pictures of his important adults, as well as specific expectations for them. For each caregiver the baby's expectations are different.

Fathers Are Important

Future research on attachment may provide fresh insights on when and how infants form an attachment to their fathers and how this evolves over time. What is clear now is that young children's relationships with their fathers and other men in their lives are very important. Children benefit when fathers are positively involved in their lives (Marsiglio et al. 2000).

In intact two-parent families as well as in single-parent households, children benefit from healthy relationships with their fathers or father figures.

Although many divorced or unmarried fathers maintain quality relationships with their children, as a group they are less likely to do so (Marsiglio et al. 2000). To contribute to children's well-being, all fathers—married, unmarried, divorced, or separated—must do more than merely be present and more than just be a goodtime playmate. They must offer emotional support and quality parenting.

Children show positive outcomes when fathers' parenting is authoritative—that is, their parenting combines nurturing with clear limits (Baumrind 1977; Amato & Gilbreth 1999). Fathers contribute to their children's well-being when they

• provide emotional support

• give everyday assistance

• monitor children's behavior

• provide noncoercive discipline (Marsiglio et al. 2000).

This type of paternal attention toward children generates

• academic success

• fewer behavior problems

• less depression, fewer self-esteem problems, more satisfaction with life

• greater social competence and more prosocial behavior (Marsiglio et al. 2000).

Research shows that parents who value attachment are more likely to have securely attached babies (Grossman et al. 1988).[1] While attachment to one or both parents makes a difference to children's later development (Matas, Arend, & Sroufe 1978; Main & Weston 1981; Sroufe & Fleeson 1986),[2] research also shows that some of children's later behaviors are tied to quality of early attachment to specifically the mother or the father. For example, children's emotional openness and verbal fluency at 6 years seem to be strongly related to the security of their attachment in infancy to the mother but unrelated to their attachment to the father (Main, Kaplan, & Cassidy 1985).[3]

In general, attachment to the mother predicts children's development after infancy better than does attachment to the father. A review of 70 studies shows that fathers shape the infant's attachment, although to a lesser extent than do mothers (van IJzendoorn & De Wolff 1997).[4] It may be that fathers' strongest influences on infant attachment are indirect rather than direct. For example, in a family with an alcoholic father, the mother may be so stressed or so fearful that she is too depressed to give the child the care and nurturance needed for healthy development. In consequence, and in an indirect way then, the father's behaviors disrupt and undermine the infant-mother relationship. Conversely, a father who provides emotional and practical support to the mother contributes to her ability to be responsive and nurturing.

Also likely is that the child's attachment to the father is influenced by different aspects from those influencing attachment to the mother. Fathers have their own ways of interacting with very young children. For example, key factors for fathers may include quality of play or encouragement of autonomy.

Suzanne's dad lies motionless on the living room floor, eyes closed, as if asleep. Suzanne toddles over and looks down at him. No movement. She bends down, braces her hands against his chest, and looks into his face. Still no movement. Then suddenly Dad opens his eyes and exclaims, "Boo!" Suzanne bursts into giggles.

We've all seen dads engage in this type of play. A father gently tosses a ball again and again to a toddler and urges him to

reach out and catch it—this too is a typical scenario. Fathers of securely attached toddlers appear to show higher sensitivity in their playful challenges with their children (at 24 months) than do fathers of insecurely attached toddlers, and this sensitivity remains consistent over the first six years of life (Grossman 1997).

Attachment at risk

Sometimes a young child is neglected or abused or receives inadequate bodily care from a distracted or disturbed parent un-

Snips and Snails and Puppy Dog Tails

Although we tend to think of baby girls as delicate and fragile, it is baby boys who in fact are most vulnerable to difficulties in attachment—at home and in care settings. Researchers found that baby boys (at 15 months) tend to receive less responsive care than girls in child care centers and in family child care homes (NICHD Early Child Care Research Network 1997). In families where both parents work outside the home, 1-year-old boys as a group receive less stimulation from their parents than girls, as well as receiving less stimulation than girls or boys reared in families with an at-home parent (Zaslow & Hayes 1986). In child care programs for families with low incomes, boy toddlers were found to show more needy behaviors, requesting more help and attention from teachers than girls. Even though they are as likely to be compliant with a teacher's request, boys tend to receive more negative teacher attention than girls (Wittmer & Honig 1987).

Differences like these alert us to rethink the stereotypes of girls and boys and to respect children's needs for love and reassurance regardless of gender. Providers need to cuddle and croon over baby boys as well as baby girls. Extra tenderness and nurturing for boys in the child care setting may help to make up for what some may lack at home.

able to tune in to his unique personality and personal needs. When a parent is addicted to alcohol or drugs, for example, the baby may learn to cope with erratic caregiving by distancing herself from the substance-abusing parent. A large percentage of maltreated infants are not securely attached to their mothers. And those who are tend to shift toward insecure attachment over time (Schneider-Rosen et al. 1985).[5] It appears that babies learn early not to seek comfort from caregivers who are unable to nurture them.

Parents who maltreat their children often were themselves maltreated in childhood. These adults tend to repeat their parents' behaviors (Kempe et al. 1962).[6] Many abusive mothers did not experience their attachment figures as being reliable and accessible (DeLozier 1982). Even with intensive therapeutic help a mother dealing with memories of her own childhood neglect or abuse may have difficulty empathizing with her baby and providing responsive, nurturing care (Fraiberg, Adelson, & Shapiro 1975).

Early childhood professionals and social workers who interact regularly with families need to be alert to the special needs of babies who do not seem to be receiving adequate care. Besides providing what support they can to the family, early childhood staff should make every effort to get the family appropriate professional help and outside supports. For example, in some communities home visitor services are available. The home visitor reaches out to a family on a regular basis, providing a model of effective and compassionate parenting to help banish the malignant "ghosts in the nursery" from a parent's traumatic past (Fraiberg, Adelson, & Shapiro 1975).

> *During a home visit a teen mother complains that her baby is very bad. When the visitor asks what the creeping baby does to upset her, the mother tells her, "She gets in the garbage." The garbage bag, filled with interesting, colorful materials such as wrappers from frozen foods, is on the kitchen floor. The mother is convinced that the baby is trying intentionally to annoy her by playing with the garbage.*
>
> *The home visitor carefully explores with the mom where else bags of garbage might be kept so that her adventurous baby does not play with them. After considering several suggestions, the mother decides to move the bag to the counter.*

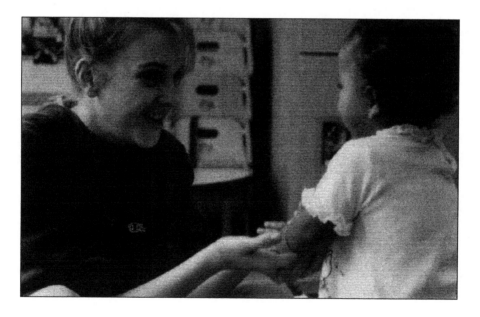

When a child is without a secure attachment at home, the child care provider becomes a crucial person indeed. For this baby, the provider who responds quickly and appropriately to his cries of distress, gives him daily baby massages after diaper changes (*Baby Massage* 1989), and holds and cuddles and sings to him often during the course of the day is nurturing his attachment to her. For a young child at risk, the provider who notices and admires her prosocial actions, holds her close to read and talk  about a picture book, and helps her negotiate entry into a group of children playing is encouraging trust and a positive relationship with a caring adult. The caregiver offers the child an opportunity to form a secure attachment to a stable, genuinely intimate, loving adult who provides in sensitive ways for the child's psychological as well as physical needs.

A secure attachment in the child care setting can be a lifesaver for an abused or neglected infant, and it is a plus for all children. If a baby is already securely attached to one or more family figures, hooray! Then the child who spends time in the early childhood program is that much richer in secure attachments.

Just as evidence shows that parental attachment has positive developmental effects for children, so too research shows positive effects of nonparental attachment on children's progress (Werner 1993; Howes 1999). Securely attached children in child care feel free to independently explore the world around them. Their positive, competent attitude gives them the confidence to take risks and solve problems.

Child care quality, family factors, and attachment

In a great many families with young children, both parents (or the single parent) work outside the home. Does out-of-home employment—specifically the mother's, since research focuses on mothers—affect children?

How children fare in child care depends significantly, of course, on how well we in early childhood positions do our jobs. Other factors can make a difference too. Is the child in care full time or part time? At what age did the child enter out-of-home care? Over time, is he in one setting or in many? How does the parent interact with the child? Effects of these factors in turn vary with family characteristics such as income level. For example, when mothers not responsive to their babies also use low-quality child care or tend to switch care arrangements, the children are less likely to form secure attachments (NICHD Early Child Care Research Network 1997). What seems to happen is that two or more risk factors add up to a measurable impact.

Early childhood teachers and administrators can better serve children and families when they are aware of available knowledge on child care effects. Five major themes from the research base are particularly important for practitioners.

More than a Clean Diaper and a Full Stomach

Not surprisingly, babies with abusive parents or other caregivers usually fail to form healthy attachments to them. But the story doesn't end there. Also at risk for insecure attachment—or no attachment at all—are children whose caregivers pay them little attention beyond caring for their physical needs.

Some caregivers, although not at all unkind, are perfunctory in their treatment of children. They treat the infants and toddlers in their care almost as objects requiring regular maintenance rather than as interesting and highly individual people.

In the well-appointed infant room, the walls are painted bright colors. Cribs are sturdy and toys are plentiful, scattered on the carpet where babies sit or crawl about. One teacher washes bibs at the sink. Another arranges diapers on a shelf.

One calls to the other, "Has that one been fed yet?"

"No, not yet. And this one needs to be diapered," responds the second teacher, nodding her head toward a baby sitting vacant-eyed on the floor.

Such a lack of connection is sometimes termed **psychological unavailability**—meaning that the caregiver takes adequate care of the baby but not does not form a relationship with him. The caregiver's psychological unavailability is dangerous, strongly predicting a baby's insecure attachment (Egeland & Sroufe 1981).[7]

High-quality care leads to positive child outcomes

Child care quality is a consistent predictor of children's behavior and social-emotional development (NICHD Early Child Care Research Network 2001). Children receiving more sensitive and responsive attention in child care tend to have fewer caregiver-reported problems at ages 2 and 3 (NICHD Early Child Care Research Network 1997, 2001). Certain aspects of child care combine with particular family factors to increase the likelihood of insecure attachment. For example, insecure attachment is more common in infants who receive poor quality care or are moved from one child care setting to another when—and only when—the mother herself is low in sensitivity (NICHD Early Child Care Research Network 1997, 2001).

Quality of child care over the first three years of life shows consistent but modest links to children's cognitive and language development (NICHD Early Child Care Research Network 2001). The higher the quality of care (that is, the more positive language stimulation and interaction there is), the greater the child's language abilities at 15, 24, and 36 months; the better the child's cognitive development at age 2; and the greater the child's school readiness at age 3. Other researchers have also found favorable cognitive outcomes of child care.

For instance, Park & Honig (1991) found that children who entered child care at a younger age were rated as higher in abstraction ability; however, they also found slightly higher aggression ratings for children who began full-time care in their first year than for those who began in the second or fourth year.

Child outcomes vary with time spent in care

Similar findings are emerging from a large-scale longitudinal study funded by the National Institute of Child Health and Human Development (NICHD Early Child Care Research Network 2001) in which investigators at 10 sites nationally are following a diverse population of 1,364 babies from birth.

This study finds mother and caregiver/teacher ratings of children's behavior to be slightly less favorable, at least at some ages, for children who have spent a lot of time in child care (Peth-Pierce 1998; NICHD Early Child Care Research Network 2001). These behaviors, however, are well within the normal range for the age group. Family characteristics—particularly the mother's sensitivity to the child—are much stronger predictors of children's behavior than is child care experience. Of particular interest to caregivers is this finding: children who receive sensitive and responsive attention in child care tend to have fewer provider-reported problems at ages 2 and 3 than do other children in care (Peth-Pierce 1998).

Caregivers influence parents and the parent-child relationship

High-quality provider-child interactions are associated with more positive mother-child interaction (NICHD Early Child Care Research Network 2001). Babies and toddlers experiencing positive interactions with caregivers get the additional benefit of their mothers tending to become more involved with them and more sensitive to their cues (NICHD Early Child Care Research Network 1997). Encouragingly, low-income mothers using full-time higher quality care show more positive involvement with their infants (at 6 months) than do mothers using lower quality full-time care or none at all (NICHD Early Child Care Research Network 1997). In high-quality child care settings children are also more positively engaged with the mother (at 36 months).

Children from stressed families are at risk

Insecure attachment may be more common in households under certain kinds of stress than in less stressed families[8]. For example, mothers' early return to work, often unavoidable in poor families, can put secure attachment at risk (Vaughn, Deane, & Waters 1985). Babies from poor, stressed families are found to fare better when mothers do not return to work until children are older. As toddlers they tend to be more cooperative, enthusiastic, and persistent at difficult tool-using tasks than children of mothers who went back to work early—even when both groups of children were securely attached at 12 months (Vaughn, Deane, & Waters 1985).

Parents need better information about and access to quality care

Unfortunately, many mothers who strongly believe that their employment benefits their children do not choose high quality care (NICHD Early Child Care Research Network 1997). Indeed, their children tend to be in poorer care and for more hours a week than do children whose mothers are more doubtful about how their employment affects their children. Clearly parents need to become better informed consumers of child care (Honig 2002). For instance, some parents may pay attention to superficial aspects of the facility rather than to the quality of caregivers' interactions with children. Some parents like the idea of rotating staff frequently among the babies rather than keeping babies with a primary caregiver. This preference stems from parents' natural though misguided concerns about a child's becoming strongly attached to a particular caregiver—parents want to be first and foremost in their babies' affections and worry that they might be displaced by the provider.

Because such fears and misunderstandings can lead parents to make poor choices, early childhood professionals need to help families learn about quality care. Having better informed parents creates two major benefits: families are better able to choose high-quality care *and* they know more about giving children sensitive care at home (Honig 2002). Both of these outcomes promote secure attachment.

Easing separation anxiety in child care

Separation anxiety is a natural part of the attachment process and children's development. Even children who have for months cheerily and comfortably gone from their parents to the child care provider may rather suddenly show great anxiety at a parent's departure. To the parent and teacher who

Preparing Parents for Separation

When a new child enters your program, you welcome her with open arms, taking a number of steps to ensure her comfort in the classroom and with her peers. Although the main focus is on the child, don't forget the parents; they too may need reassurance. Remember, parents are likely to be feeling anxiety or guilt upon leaving their child in a new care setting or being apart from her for the first time.

It's important to talk about separation before the big day arrives. Discuss strategies at a parent orientation, during a home visit, or in a parent-teacher conference. Parents can discuss their role, how they can prepare the child at home, and what to expect the first week. Also have a written statement on the program's separation policy for parents to read at their leisure. Encourage them to talk to other parents about their feelings; they will be relieved to find that they are not alone.

Good caregiver-family relationships are essential to good child care. As you establish rapport with parents their anxiety will decrease. Demonstrate from the beginning your willingness to learn from them and work with them on their child's behalf. And tell parents often how important they are in their child's life.

thought everything was progressing smoothly, these bouts or crying and leg clinging can be a disturbing jolt.

Separation anxiety typically starts when children are about 8 months old; it peaks between 10 and 18 months and winds down by the end of the second year (Ramsburg 1998). Separation anxiety is evidenced by a baby's increased anxiety and fear in meeting new people and entering new situations as well as by his intensified clinging behavior.

Clinging and crying upon separation from a parent or familiar caregiver is normal during this period. These behaviors reflect the child's attachment. Babies do not comprehend that a person who leaves their sight will come back, or that the person may only have walked into the next room. Understanding separation anxiety helps parents and caregivers to be patient and sympathetic with children during this difficult period (Ramsburg 1998).

Take It Easy

Children and parents both need time to adjust to a new care setting. One of the best ways to help families make the transition is to encourage them to come on board slowly, through a process of gradual enrollment (Miller & Albrecht 2000, 39–40).

Enrolling gradually means that a family member and the child together spend the first week getting to know you and becoming familiar with the classroom for a little while each day. For the first few days the parent and child visit for a couple of hours, each day staying a little longer, with the parent perhaps leaving the room for some of the time when the child seems comfortable. By the end of the week the child should be ready to spend the day in the care setting with a minimum of discomfort without the family member present.

This process entails a certain amount of inconvenience for working parents. Some use flex time to accommodate the gradual enrollment process. Others may turn to a close family member—a grandparent, for example—to help with the classroom visits or to care for the child later in the day. Encourage parents who are tight on time to spend at least the first two days visiting the classroom with the child.

Parents may be more eager to participate in gradual enrollment when they understand how important it is for their child's well-being. Explain that their infant or toddler will have a much easier time adapting to the new environment when mom or dad is nearby for comfort and support. This initial getting-to-know-you period also helps acquaint parents with classroom routines and allows them to see the program's philosophy in action.

Begin your relationship with the children in your care and their parents the best way—one day at a time.

Every child experiences separation differently based on variations in temperament and life experience. Individual children may experience separation anxiety at different times and at varying levels; children under stress from a move, a change of child care providers, or some other event that disrupts their routine may experience more separation anxiety than others. When providers work with families to help children and parents ease the separations that are part of child care, they support the security of children's attachment relationships. Children learn that leaving the beloved parent does not have to be heartrending. They also learn that while separating means leaving someone special, it may also mean going to another comforting adult.

Providers can use a variety of strategies to ease the stress of separation, beginning with preparing the parents (see "Preparing Parents for Separation"). One strategy that works for parents and child is a gradual enrollment process (see "Take It Easy"). Encouraging parents to establish a separation ritual, such as blowing kisses to the child, is a good idea. Likewise a ritual for pickup time smoothes the parent-child reunion later in the day. Parents need to understand that sneaking out on a child while his attention is diverted—a common ploy to avoid upset in the morning—just adds to separation problems. Consider this experience from the child's point of view:

> Imagine how you would feel if you looked up from the blocks you were stacking or the fish you were helping feed to find that the person you depend on most in the world, one of your parents, had disappeared with no warning. Chances are, you would begin to feel as if you had to keep alert: if your mother or father can disappear so quickly, the world isn't such a safe place. What might happen next? When will they come back and when will they leave again? It would be difficult to relax even when they were there because you'd never be sure when they might vanish again. (Dombro & Bryan 1991, 96)

Other approaches to easing separation include bringing in comfort items from home, such as a stuffed animal, favorite toy, or cherished blanket that a child can cuddle with if she feels sad, and having family photos available— in cubbies, on a bulletin board, in little photo albums—that a child can look at when she is missing the parent. Parents can also tape record a greeting, favorite song, or story for the child to listen to during the day to ease the gnawing aches of longing.

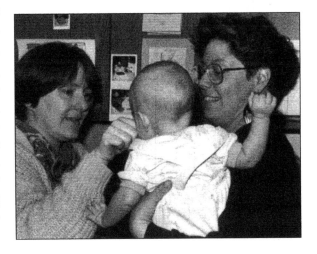

Building a Partnership with Parents

There are many ways to bridge the gap between family and child care. Here are some tried-and-true ideas for fostering working partnerships with parents.

• Provide a notebook for parents to communicate with you. Create a routine way for parents to let you know their concerns when there is no opportunity to talk at drop-off or pickup times. Place a large book and a pencil near the classroom entry, with each child's name at the top of a page. Then a parent can scribble hurriedly a concern, such as a baby having slept fitfully the previous night because of teething.

• Make your child care facility family-friendly. Be supportive of breastfeeding mothers and parents stopping by to spend time with their infants. Have a comfortable chair or a quiet place where a father on his lunch break can feed and cuddle his infant or a mother can nurse her baby.

• Keep in touch through notes to home. Send home brief, positive notes on a regular basis offering a glimpse into the child's development. "Jimmy and Lauren played side by side in the sandbox and jabbered away. They are good friends." "Tony tried a bit of broccoli today at lunch." "Carlos pointed to a dog in a picture book today." "Jeremy was helpful on the playground, patting Hoagy's hair when Hoagy fell down and cried."

One qualification here: Parents naturally want to witness their child's first steps and hear the child's first word. Let parents tell *you* about those thrills, even though you may have noticed such treasured milestones yourself. Rejoice with the proud parent.

Parent-caregiver relations and attachment

The relationship between provider and parent affects the child's attachment to both. A supportive parent-caregiver relationship strengthens a child's attachment to the caregiver and his comfort in the setting, as he picks up the message that his mother values this person and trusts her to take care of him. When his parent shows confidence in the caregiver and the setting, the child is more likely to feel confident as well.

Caregivers likewise should communicate their respect for the parents. Children's major human resources are their parents, and providers and teachers should convey to parents how deeply important they are in helping their children thrive. Many parents are stressed; they may be worried about money, health, jobs, or personal relationships. They appreciate the caregiver's affirming how very special they are to their child.

Interviews (Baker & Manfredi-Petitt 1998) with family child care providers reveal some interesting thoughts about relationships with parents: "It's easy for caregivers to fall into the trap of feeling that they are doing everything right and that parents are doing everything wrong," states one. Another observes, "Parent-provider relationships make or break the business. Parents don't come into your home like a friend or a relative. They're clients. You have to bend and be flexible. You can't be cut-and-dried in your judgments." A third provider reflects that "it is important to set limits for yourself by respecting parents as heads of their own household" (p. 35).

When program practices emphasize continuity of care (see Chapter 2, p. 22), parents and caregivers have time to become more comfortable with each other. As they watch the child grow from infancy through toddlerhood, they share an awareness of the child's temperament and individual needs. This allows parents and caregivers to plan and work together to

address those needs, devising strategies to use at home and in child care and keeping one another apprised of changes or progress in particular areas.

Joseph Stone's (1973a, 1973b) classic films on infant-toddler care in Israeli kibbutzim dramatically convey how well children do when parents and caregivers have a good relationship. In the films we can see how comfortable infants feel when their mothers hand them over each morning to a *metapelet* (caregiver) who is also a close family friend. The secure ease of this transition is in marked contrast to the difficulties some infants experience daily in separating from their parents to go to child care providers who are virtual strangers to the family.

Researchers are only beginning to explore the significance of the parent-provider relationship in infant development. However, in programs for infants and toddlers, it seems that policies and practices that promote communication and rapport between providers and parents are likely to allay parents' anxiety and promote the security of infants' attachments to both caregivers and parents (Noppe, Elicker, & Fortner-Wood 1998).

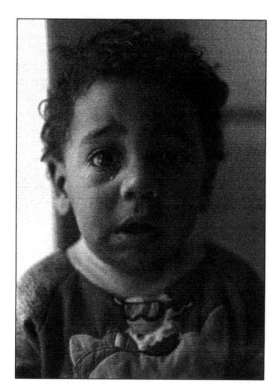

Sometimes parents turn to the caregiver for advice, pouring out their troubles, which can place the caregiver in an uncomfortable position. Having a sympathetic listener and hearing a few words of comfort, understanding, or common sense may be all the parent needs in such situations. But when providers feel inadequate to address problems parents present, they should have on hand information about community resources to guide parents to agencies that can help with family problems.

At other times caregivers may feel they are pitted against par-

Secure Relationships

When Caregivers and Parents Don't Agree

When you and parents disagree, there are usually three courses of action you can take. You can let an issue go—that is, ignore it. You can choose to face the problem and work it out. Or you can decide things are unworkable and end the relationship.

Differences can often stir up feelings of frustration and anger. These feelings can make it difficult to resolve problems. Try to be aware of issues that are "hot spots" for you. Recognizing what they are may help you deal with them before they become a problem. Sometimes, talking with co-workers who have had similar experiences can help you understand a situation and may give you ideas of how to work with families toward a resolution. Here are some principles that may help guide you through the process of attempting to resolve conflicts.

• Keep the children's best interests in mind. Children need you and their families to deal with your differences in ways that don't interfere with their care.

• Let parents know you understand their feelings. Often the issues that come up generate strong feelings. Just acknowledging that you understand can put parents at ease.

• Build on your history together. A disagreement doesn't have to mean that one of you is doing something wrong. Instead, a disagreement can be a point from which both you and families can learn and grow.

• Have realistic expectations. Resolving differences often takes much time and discussion. Some differences may never be resolved. However, as long as you both are willing to discuss an issue, your relationship with families and your support of the child can continue.

Reprinted with permission from A.L. Dombro, L.J. Colker, & D.T. Dodge, *The Creative Curriculum for Infants & Toddlers* (Washington, DC: Teaching Strategies, rev. ed., 1999), pp. 29–30.

ents in determining the best course of action for a child. Differences of opinion between parents and teachers do occur. One parent worries that the child is growing too attached to his teacher. Another parent wants the family child care provider to take away the bottle from a baby who still has strong sucking needs. Or perhaps a parent whose toddler does not sleep through the night tells the provider not to allow the child to

Signs of a Young Child's Trust in Your Caregiving

Developing a bond between you and the babies, toddlers, or young children in your care is one of your major goals. You act quickly and warmly to comply with their needs, and you temper your responses to their individual styles. You show respect to children and shower them with praise in the wake of their good deeds. You use contingent feedback to support or alter their behaviors. You talk to them, hold them, hug them, read to them, and smile across the room at them. You communicate and work with their families in the interest of the children's well-being.

How can you tell when you have succeeded in forming a strong bond with a child? When the child

• smiles with pleasure when you greet her warmly or admire her accomplishments

• reaches out to you to be picked up

• calls out to you to get your attention

• relaxes and molds comfortably to your body when you hold her

• leans into your body when you read to him

• accepts your gentle touches and warm gestures of intimacy

• climbs on you, clings to you, or even sucks on your knuckles to regain emotional balance

• looks up occasionally to check for your presence when playing across the room

• becomes stressed when he notices you are not in the room

• runs to you, her safe base, to "refuel," then returns to play

• turns to you for help in stressful situations

• takes your hand in new or unfamiliar circumstances

• calms down at your reassuring touch and words

• is cooperative and compliant with your requests and directions

• works longer at challenging tasks when you are near

• looks into your eyes when you crouch down to talk to him

• talks to you truthfully about the bad as well as the good

When babies and young children show a number of these behaviors, they are well along in forming a secure attachment to you, their warm, responsive, and reliable caregiver. And you have given them a gift that will serve them for a lifetime.

nap, although the provider believes he still needs a naptime. Sometimes a difference of opinion can be traced to cultural differences or a lack of understanding about child development; however, parents also have knowledge about their children that providers do not have (Bredekamp & Copple 1997). Respect between caregiver and parents and a deep desire to work out problems—the fruits of a strong parent-teacher partnership—are the best foundation for negotiating such differences.

Conclusion

Attachment is the emotional glue that bonds children to the important people in their lives. For most children, the primary caregiver—the child's mother—is the crucial attachment figure. The mother-child relationship brings safety, comfort, and pleasure to the infant. It also sets the stage for relationships with others throughout life. While paternal attachment is vitally important, research shows a more direct correlation between maternal attachment and later development. When the child is not securely attached to either parent, the role of the caregiver becomes crucial. Children are served best when teachers and parents partner to support attachment.

Attachment patterns in infancy are often hard to change as children grow because home life situations do not tend to change, whether they are loving and nurturing or neglectful and harsh. The latter can cause children to experience later difficulties in relationships with peers and with teachers. However, a determined, insightful, and skilled provider or teacher can act in ways that help an infant or young child develop a secure relationships with her.

The wonderful news about attachment is that the relationships built up between a baby or a young child and each of his caregivers are unique. Any child care provider can be that special person who awakens and nurtures in a child a special sense of being loved and being worthy of love. This is an awesome responsibility and one that can engender great pride in the adult who provides such care.

Closing Thoughts for You, the Caregiver

Most of us have some stressful memories from childhood. Some of us received ample support and nurturing as children; others little to none. But whatever our baggage, all of us can benefit personally and professionally from reflecting on our past.

Through reflection, determination, and hard work an individual can change his or her internalized working model. If you experienced a harsh upbringing, you can decide never to punish physically, never to neglect, never to be overly controlling with a baby or young child as your parents were with you. In the same way, reflection can help free a new parent to treat a new baby thoughtfully and tenderly (Brophy-Herb & Honig 1999). An adult or teenager's ability and desire to think about the difficult or inappropriate parenting she experienced as a child can galvanize and motivate her. The more we recognize our strengths, limits, fears, and joys, the better we are able to act calmly and thoughtfully under stress and handle daily challenges in relating to young children.

Maybe you have worked hard to develop a secure relationship with a toddler in your care, only to face the jealousy of an insecure parent. Sometimes you feel exasperated with the behaviors of children who seem to know how to push your buttons. Or you may be confronted with a child who once again has acted aggressively toward another. Finding reassuring words to allay a parent's insecurities, taking a moment to analyze a situation and come up with a new approach, showing understanding when children's negative feelings result in hurtful actions—these constructive responses require patience, thought, and self-possession.

You can respond with maturity and calm only when you are in tune with your own feelings. Tired, stressed-out caregivers need a friend or sympathetic co-worker to whom they can voice their difficult emotions. When you feel a sense of loss after a child in your group moves to another setting, turn to a trusted adult to discuss your feelings. Sharing feelings lightens stress and helps prevent teacher burnout.

Expressing yourself more openly, voicing your honest and sometimes complex feelings to another will help you clarify your thinking and find the strength to reach out to a child with difficult behaviors or a parent who tries your patience. Reflect on yourself and your relationships with intimate others in your life, past and the present. Nurture yourself. Cultivate supportive, caring friendships.

If you belong to a faith community, you may find there the strength and renewal of spirit to go into the classroom daily and maintain the caring atmosphere and intimate interactions with children that form the strong fabric of secure attachment. These steps can help you develop the inner resources to become a nurturing teacher, building a positive attachment with each child in your care. We may not be able to "save" every young child for whom we provide care. Some children's lives are too full of neglect or brutality. Yet we can always try and try again to extend loving kindness toward each child.

Endnotes

Introduction

1. A method called the Waters Q-Sort is commonly used to measure attachment in older toddlers and preschoolers. The Q-Sort consists of 100 items, each printed on a small card, that assess the attachment, exploration, and related behaviors of a young child in the home and other naturalistic settings from the child's world of experiences. A caregiver or other knowledgeable professional who has observed the child extensively sorts the cards into piles ranging from *very like* to *very unlike* the child. The items refer to specific behaviors, such as

- When upset, child sits and cries; does not go to mother
- Follows mother's suggestions readily
- Often cries, resists going to bed or sleep
- Rarely asks for help when upset
- Would rather play with toys than adults
- Acts sorry or ashamed if mother speaks firmly
- Asks mother for hugs or cuddle
- Easily becomes angry with mother

A full explanation of the procedure and the security criterion for assessment can be found on the Internet at www.psychology.sunysb.edu/ewaters/measures/aqs.htm.

2. The Adult Attachment Interview (AAI) (Main & Goldwyn, in press) is a procedure for assessing adults' strategies for identifying, preventing, and protecting the self from perceived dangers, particularly dangers tied to intimate relationships. Four AAI response patters categorize an adult's state of mind with respect to attachment: autonomous, dismissing, preoccupied, and unresolved.

Adults classified as *autonomous* are generally thoughtful, value attachment experiences and relationships, and freely examine the effects of past experiences on personal development. *Dismissing* persons discount attachment experiences as unimportant for their own development and in raising their children. Often they cannot remember early events, and they tend to either idealize or disparage their parents. *Preoccupied* adults are enmeshed in their early experiences and family relationships, although they have trouble relating a coherent story of their childhood. They may still be dependent on, angry at, or trying overmuch to please their parents. Adults classified as *unresolved* seem confused and disoriented when discussing experiences in their past of abuse or loss of a loved one.

Studies using the AAI and Strange Situation techniques show a high correspondence between patterns of maternal response to the AAI and their infants' responses to the Strange Situation (Fonagy, Steele, & Steele 1991).

Chapter 1: Understanding Attachment

1. Self-regulation is fundamental to a baby's ability to share in the emotional reciprocity of the growing positive relationship with a nurturing adult. By serving as a resource for babies' self-regulation, caregivers ensure that the babies in their care can participate in the process of developing a secure attachment.

Researchers (Block & Block 1980) found that kindergarten children who were assessed in infancy as securely attached showed more ego resiliency and ego control—that is, they adapted more flexibly to changing circumstances and showed more ability to regulate their own strong emotions—than did children who had been observed to be insecurely attached infants.

2. Current research (Bower 2000) at the Institute of Psychiatry in London has increased knowledge about the effects of deprivation in early life. Observation of 111 infants and young children from Romanian orphanages and interviews with their adoptive parents reveal that children exposed to the most severe deprivation have the highest rates of attachment disorder. The rate of attachment disorder among the Romanian infants adopted by age 6 months was 7%; for those adopted between 6 and 24 months, 21%; and 31% for children adopted between 2 and 3½ years.

The children with attachment disorder showed indiscriminate friendliness, disregarding their adoptive parents and eagerly approaching strangers. Nor did they turn to their parents in new or scary situations. They often misinterpreted social cues and showed only a superficial interest in others. Children who have spent their first few years "without affectionate care [or] sensory stimulation . . . often can't form close relationships" (Bower 2000, 343).

These data send a clear message. The degree and length of deprivation of stability and love a baby suffers during the infant/toddler period make a difference in her later adjustment. The longer the period before babies were adopted, the higher the rate of attachment disorder. This tells us that babies who are in temporary placement because their families could not provide for them or were abusive or neglectful cannot be allowed to languish in limbo. Warm, dependable adult care is powerfully important in the earliest years.

3. How is security of attachment assessed? Mary Ainsworth's Strange Situation technique, used at 12 and 18 months, has become the major measure for determining infant attachment. In this procedure the mother (or other attachment figure) and the infant enter a playroom equipped with engaging toys. For three-minute intervals the baby is in the room first with the mother, then with a stranger, then reunited with the mother, then alone, then again with the stranger, and finally reunited again with the mother. From careful analysis of the infant's reunion behaviors with the mother, researchers note different attachment patterns.

Chapter 2: Attachment to Early Childhood Caregivers

1. Here are some resources describing positive guidance techniques for caregivers:

> Martha B. Bronson, "Research in Review: Recognizing and Supporting the Development of Self-Regulation in Young Children" [article]—in *Young Children* (March 2000), vol. 55, no. 2; available from IDS of Thomson Scientific Corp., 215-386-0100, ext. 4900 (e-mail ids@isinet.com).

> Thomas Gordon, *P.E.T.—Parent Effectiveness Training* [book, out of print]—look for this book at your local library or order a used copy on the Internet (www.amazon.com).

> Polly Greenberg, *Character Development: Encouraging Self-Esteem and Self-Discipline in Infants, Toddlers, and Two-Year-Olds*, 1991 [book]—available from NAEYC, Washington, D.C. (www.naeyc.org).

Alice Sterling Honig, *Behavior Guidance for Infants and Toddlers*, 1996 [book]—available from the Southern Early Childhood Association, Little Rock, Arkansas (www.seca50.org).

Alice Sterling Honig, *Love and Learn: Positive Guidance for Young Children*, 2000 [brochure]—available from NAEYC, Washington, D.C. (www.naeyc.org).

Ronald G. Slaby, W.C. Roedell, D. Arezzo, & K. Hendrix, *Early Violence Prevention: Tools for Teachers of Young Children*, 1995 [book]—available from NAEYC, Washington, D.C. (www.naeyc.org).

Jeannette Galambos Stone, *A Guide to Discipline*, 1978 (rev. ed.) [book]—available from NAEYC, Washington, D.C. (www.naeyc.org).

2. Matas, Arend, and Sroufe (1978) observed young children (age 30 months) who at 12 and 18 months had been classified as securely, avoidantly, or ambivalently attached. The children were playing with intriguing new toys. When instructed after a short time to put the toys away, all showed frustration and reluctance. Next, with their mothers present, the toddlers faced tool-using tasks too difficult to perform without adult help. For example, in one task the child was to retrieve a treat using a six-foot lever. Children rated as securely attached were zestful in tackling the hard tasks, cooperative, and compliant with their mothers' suggestions. In contrast, those who had been classified as insecurely attached tended to cry, have temper tantrums, or not comply with their mothers' suggestions, giving up rather than persisting with the problem. For their part these mothers gave fewer helpful suggestions than did the mothers of the securely attached toddlers.

Chapter 3: Parents, Caregivers, and Attachment in Child Care

1. In a study in Germany (Grossman et al. 1988), an attachment-valuing representation among mothers was associated with secure Strange Situation scores for their babies. Representations that devalued attachment were found among mothers of 13 of 15 insecurely attached infants. The mothers of babies classified as secure were open and sympathetic in discussing attachment issues despite memories of problematic and unsupportive parents. The mothers of babies classified as insecure revealed "memories of unsupportive attachment figures, little thinking, and strong avoidance of attachment-related issues" (Grossman & Grossman 1990, 44).

2. Some research has shown infancy attachment to have a powerful relationship to later interactions of preschoolers with peers and teachers. Sroufe and Fleeson (1986, 1988) paired up preschoolers as playmates according to the children's infancy attachment classifications. When those rated as avoidant were paired with children rated as ambivalent, the latter bore sarcasm, derision, and rejection by their playmates. When two children classified in infancy as ambivalent played together, they showed immaturity and social ineptitude but not exploitation; such children were often isolated in the classroom. Securely attached children playing with each other were neither victimizers nor victims.

The preschool teachers, who did not know the children's infancy attachment ratings, gave more leeway for misbehavior and more nurturance to children rated as ambivalent. They sometimes got angry—but only with children rated as avoidant. With these children, teachers were highly controlling and had lower expectations for cooperative behavior. Teachers were least nurturing toward children who had been classified as secure and had the highest expectations for compliance for them.

3. In a study by Main, Kaplan, and Cassidy (1985), 6-year-olds were told, "This little boy's [girl's] parents are going away on vacation for two weeks. What's this little boy [girl] going to do?" Children's constructive responses included calling on people to help or actively trying to persuade the parents not to go. These constructive responses correlated ($r = .59$) with children's secure attachment as babies to mothers, but barely at all with secure attachment to fathers ($r = .14$).

When presented with a family photograph, secure 6-year-olds smiled, showed some interest, then put it aside. Those who had been insecurely attached babies responded in disorganized ways. The 6-year-olds' responses to the family photo correlated ($r = .74$) with their Strange Situation attachment status in infancy with mothers but was not significantly related to how they had been attached to fathers five years earlier.

4. In their review, van IJzendoorn and De Wolff (1997) found a strong correlation ($r = .50$) between the mother's attachment representation and the baby's attachment to her; for fathers the correlation was $r = .37$.

5. Using the Strange Situation procedure, Schneider-Rosen and colleagues (1985) found that at 18 months, 46% of abused babies were

classified as avoidant, 23% secure, and 31% anxious resistant. In contrast, the babies in the nonmaltreated group were rated 7% avoidant, 67% secure, and 26% anxious resistant. Stability of attachment between 12 and 18 months was higher for the nonmaltreated babies (69%) than for the maltreated (41%). No clear relationship was found between type of maltreatment and quality of attachment.

6. According to Kempe and colleagues, "The child is seen as the reincarnation of the caregiver's bad self, for which he was punished when he was a child, prompting the caregiver to shift his identification to his own punitive caregiver's and to punish the child with a sense of full justification" (1962, 90–91).

7. Among babies whose mothers were psychologically unavailable, Egeland and Sroufe (1981) found that at 12 months 43% were rated avoidant, but at 18 months 86% were rated avoidant. The others were rated ambivalent/hesitant.

8. Stresses that impinge on families and children can be of many types. Some are acute, as when a child has to be hospitalized suddenly. Some are long term, as with a child living with an abusive alcoholic parent who flies into rages (Honig 1986a).

Internal stress can arise from babies' vulnerabilities at birth, such as prematurity, the effects of maternal drug abuse during pregnancy, or genetic anomalies like Down syndrome. Other stresses arise from the environment—living in a dangerous neighborhood where children are exposed to violence and cannot play outdoors. Some children undergo terrible stress due to the loss of a family member or their family's fleeing starvation, war, or other calamities. Others suffer stress caused by a sibling who is aggressive or whom parents clearly favor. Sometimes children sense that their parents would have preferred a child of a different sex, for example, or a more athletic child. The parents show their disappointment, leaving the child feeling rejected, bewildered, angry, or frustrated.

The role of marital conflict and external stressors as well as the effects of separation and loss after infancy should be taken into account. We need a broader, family-systems perspective on the stability and predictive power of infant attachment (Kestenbaum 1984; Sroufe 1989; Stevenson-Hinde 1990; Cowan 1997).

References

Ainsworth, M.D.S. 1967. *Infancy in Uganda: Infant care and the growth of love.* Baltimore: Johns Hopkins University Press.

Ainsworth, M.D.S. 1973. The development of infant-mother attachment. In *Review of child development research, volume 3: Child development and social policy,* eds. B.M. Caldwell & H.N. Ricciuti. Chicago: University of Chicago Press.

Ainsworth, M., & S. Bell. 1974. Mother-infant interaction and the development of competence. In *The growth of competence,* eds. K.J. Connelly & J. Brunner, 97–118. London and New York: Academic.

Ainsworth, M.D.S., M.V. Bell, & D.J. Stayton. 1971. Individual differences in the Strange Situation behavior of one-year-olds. In *The origins of human social relations,* ed. H.R. Schaffer. London: Academic.

Ainsworth, M.D.S., M.V. Bell, & D.J. Stayton. 1972. Individual differences in the development of some attachment behaviors. *Merrill-Palmer Quarterly* 18: 123–43.

Amato, P.R., & J. Gilbreth. 1999. Nonresident fathers and children's well-being: A meta-analysis. *Journal of Marriage and the Family* 61: 557–73.

Arend, R., F.L. Gove, & L.A. Sroufe. 1979. Continuity of individual adaptation from infancy to kindergarten: A predictive study of ego resiliency and curiosity in preschoolers. *Child Development* 50: 950–59.

Baby massage and exercise. 1989. Directed by Patrick Morel. 30 min. Chicago: Activideo. Videocassette.

Baker, A.C., & L.A. Manfredi-Petitt. 1998. *Circle of love: Relationships between parents, providers, and children in family child care.* St. Paul, MN: Redleaf.

Baumrind, D. 1977. Some thoughts about child rearing. In *Child development: Contemporary perspectives*, eds. S. Cohen & T.J. Comiskey, 248–58. Itasca, IL: Peacock.

Belsky, J. 1988. The "effects" of infant day care reconsidered. *Early Childhood Research Quarterly* 3: 235–72.

Belsky, J. 1996. Parent, infant, and social-contextual antecedents of father-son attachment security. *Developmental Psychology* 32: 905–13.

Belsky, J., & T. Nezworski, eds. 1988. *Clinical implications of attachments*. Hillsdale, NJ: Erlbaum.

Belsky, J., M. Rovine, & D.G. Taylor. 1984. The Pennsylvania Infant and Family Development Project, part 3. The origins of individual differences in infant-mother attachment: Maternal and infant contributions. *Child Development* 55: 718–28.

Bemporad, J.R. 1984. From attachment to affiliation. *American Journal of Psychoanalysis* 44 (1): 79–92.

Benoit, D., & K.C.H. Parker. 1994. Stability and transmission of attachment across three generations. *Child Development* 65: 1444–56.

Block, J.H., & J. Block. 1980. The role of ego-control and ego-resiliency in the organization of behavior. In *Development of cognition and social relations*, ed. W.A. Collins, 39–101. Vol. 13 in *The Minnesota symposia on child development*. Hillsdale, NJ: Erlbaum.

Bower, B. 2000. Attachment disorder draws a closer look. *Science News* 157 (22): 343.

Bowlby, J. 1958. The nature of the child's tie to its mother. *International Journal of Psychoanalysis* 39: 350–73.

Bowlby, J. [1969] 2000. *Attachment*. Vol. 1 in *Attachment and loss*. New York: Basic.

Bowlby, J. [1973] 2000. *Separation: Anxiety and anger*. Vol. 2 in *Attachment and loss*. New York: Basic.

Bowlby, J. [1980] 2000. *Loss: Sadness and depression*. Vol. 3 in *Attachment and loss*. New York: Basic.

Braungart-Rieker, J.M., M.M. Garwood, B.P. Power, & X. Wang. 2001. Parental sensitivity, infant affect, and affect regulation: Predictors of later attachment. *Child Development* 72 (1): 252–70.

Brazelton, T.B., & B.G. Cramer. 1990. *The earliest relationship: Parents, infants, and the drama of early attachment*. Reading, MA: Addison-Wesley.

Bredekamp, S., & C. Copple, eds. 1997. *Developmentally appropriate practice in early childhood programs*. Rev. ed. Washington, DC: NAEYC.

Bretherton, I. 1991. Pouring new wine into old bottles: The social self as internal working model. In *Self-processes and development*, eds. M.R. Gunnar & L.A. Sroufe, 1–4. Vol. 23 in *The Minnesota symposia on child development*. Hillsdale, NJ: Erlbaum.

Bretherton, I., & E. Waters, eds. 1985. *Growing points of attachment theory and research*. Monographs of the Society for Research in Child Development, vol. 50, nos. 1–2, serial no. 209. Chicago: University of Chicago Press.

Brophy-Herb, H.E., & A.S. Honig. 1999. Reflectivity: Key ingredient in positive adolescent parenting. *Journal of Primary Parenting* 19 (3): 24–50.

Bus, A.G., J. Belsky, M.H. van IJzendoorn, & K. Crnic. 1997. Attachment and bookreading patterns: A study of mothers, fathers, and their toddlers. *Early Childhood Research Quarterly* 12: 81–98.

Caldera, Y.M., A. Huston, & M. O'Brien. 1995. Antecedents of father-infant attachment: A longitudinal study. Paper presented at the Biennial Meeting of the Society for Research in Child Development, April, in Indianapolis, Indiana.

Cassidy, J., & P.R. Shaver, eds. 1999. *Handbook of attachment: Theory, research, and clinical applications*. New York: Guilford.

Colin, V.L. 1996. *Human attachment*. Philadelphia, PA: Temple University Press.

Commins, D.B. 1967. *Lullabies of the world*. New York: Random House.

Cowan, P. 1997. Beyond meta-analysis: A plea for a family systems view of attachment. *Child Development* 68 (4): 601–03.

Crary, E., & S.C. Steelsmith. 1996. *When you're happy and you know it*. Seattle, WA: Parenting.

Crockenberg, S.B. 1981. Infant irritability, mother responsiveness, and social support influences on the security of infant-mother attachment. *Child Development* 52: 213–22.

Crowell, J.A., & R. Waters. 1994. Bowlby's theory grown up: The role of attachment in adult love relationships. *Psychological Inquiry* 5: 31–34.

DeLozier, P.P. 1982. Attachment theory and child abuse. In *The place of attachment in human behavior*, eds. C.M. Parkes & J. Stevenson-Hinde. New York: Basic.

De Wolff, M.S., & M.H. van IJzendoorn. 1997. Sensitivity and attachment: A meta-analysis on parental antecedents of infant attachment. *Child Development* 68: 571–91.

Dombro, A.L., & P. Bryan. 1991. *Sharing the caring: How to find the right child care and make it work for you and your child.* New York: Simon & Schuster.

Dombro, A.L., L.J. Colker, & D.T. Dodge. 1999. *The creative curriculum for infants and toddlers.* Rev. ed. Washington, DC: Teaching Strategies.

Duncan, S. 1997. Be warm, loving, and responsive to your children. Available online from Montana State University Communication Services: www.montana.edu/wwwpb/home/101597fa.html (29 January 2002).

Easterbrooks, M.A., & W.A. Goldberg. 1990. Security of toddler-parent attachment: Relation to children's sociopersonal functioning during kindergarten. In *Attachment in the preschool years: Theory, research, and intervention,* eds. M.T. Greenberg, D. Cicchetti, & E.M. Cummings, 221–72. Chicago: University of Chicago Press.

Egeland, B., & L.A. Sroufe. 1981. Attachment and early maltreatment. *Child Development* 52: 44–52.

Elicker, J., M. Englund, & L.A. Sroufe. 1992. Predicting peer competence and peer relationships in childhood from early parent-child relationships. In *Family-peer relationships: Models of linkage,* eds. R. Parke & G. Ladd, 77–106. Hillsdale, NJ: Erlbaum.

Erikson, E.H. [1950] 1993. *Childhood and society.* New York: Norton.

Erickson, M.F., J. Korfmacher, & B. Egeland. 1992. Attachments past and present: Implications for therapeutic intervention with mother-infant dyads. *Development and Psychopathology* 4 (4): 495–507.

Essa, E., K. Favre, G. Thweatt, & S. Waugh. 1999. Continuity of care for infants and toddlers. *Early Child Development and Care* 148: 11–19.

Fox, N.A., M.L. Kimmerly, & W.D. Schafer. 1991. Attachment to mother/attachment to father: A meta-analysis. *Child Development* 62: 210–25.

Fraiberg, S., E. Adelson, & V. Shapiro. 1975. Ghosts in the nursery: A psychoanalytical approach to the problems of impaired infant-mother relationships. *Journal of the American Academy of Child Psychiatry* 14: 387–422.

Greenspan, S.I. 1990. *Floor time: Tuning in to each child*. New York: Scholastic. Videocassette.

Grossman, K. 1997. Infant-father attachment relationship: Sensitive challenges during play with toddler is the pivotal feature. Poster presentation at the Biennial Meeting of the Society for Research in Child Development, April, in Washington, D.C.

Grossman, K.E., E. Fremmer-Bombik, J. Rudolph, & K.E. Grossman. 1988. Maternal attachment representations as related to patterns of infant-mother attachment and maternal care during the first year. In *Relationships within families: Mutual influences*, eds. R.A. Hinde & J. Stevenson-Hinde, 241–60. Oxford, UK: Oxford Science Publications.

Grossman, K.E., & K. Grossman. 1990. The wider concept of attachment in cross-cultural research. *Human Development* 33: 31–47.

Hazan, C., & P. Shaver. 1987. Romantic love conceptualized as an attachment process. *Journal of Personality and Social Psychology* 52: 511–24.

Hesse, E., & M. Main. 2000. Disorganized infant, child, and adult attachment: Collapse in behavior and attachment strategies. *Journal of the Psychoanalytic Association* 48 (4).

Honig, A.S. 1982. Research in Review. Infant-mother communication. *Young Children* 37 (3): 52–62.

Honig, A.S. 1984. Secure attachment: Key to infant mental health. *Infant Mental Health Journal* 9 (2): 181–83.

Honig, A.S. 1985a. Research in Review. Compliance, control and discipline—Part 1. *Young Children* 40 (2): 50–58.

Honig, A.S. 1985b. Research in Review. Compliance, control, and discipline—Part 2. *Young Children* 40 (3): 47–52.

Honig, A.S. 1986a. Stress and coping in children—Part 1. *Young Children* 41 (4): 50–63.

Honig, A.S. 1986b. Stress and coping in children—Part 2. *Young Children* 41 (5): 47–59.

Honig, A.S. 1988. Research in Review. Humor development in children. *Young Children* 43 (4): 60–73.

Honig, A.S. 1989. Quality infant/toddler caregiving: Are there magic recipes? *Young Children* 44 (4): 4–10.

Honig, A.S. 1992. Dancing with your baby means sometimes leading, sometimes following. *Dimensions of Early Childhood* 20 (3): 10–13.

Honig, A.S. 1993. Mental health for babies: What do theory and research teach us? *Young Children* 48 (3): 69–76.

Honig, A.S. 1995. Singing with infants and toddlers. *Young Children* 50 (5): 72–78.

Honig, A.S. 1997. Infant temperament and personality: What do we need to know? *Montessori Life* 9 (3): 18–21.

Honig, A.S. 2000a. Cross-cultural study of infant and toddler development. In *Human development in cross-cultural perspective,* eds. A. Comunian & U. Gielen. Padua: Cedam.

Honig, A.S. 2000b. Psychosexual development in infants and young children. *Young Children* 55 (5): 70–77.

Honig, A.S. 2002. Choosing child care for young children. In *Handbook of parenting,* 2d ed., vol. 5, ed. M. Bornstein, 375–405. Hillsdale, NJ: Erlbaum.

Honig, A.S., & H.E. Brophy. 1996. *Talking with your baby: Family as the first school.* Syracuse, NY: Syracuse University Press.

Honig, A.S., & J.R. Lally. 1981. *Infant caregiving: A design for training.* Syracuse, NY: Syracuse University Press.

Honig, A.S., & A. Thompson. 1994. Helping toddlers with peer group entry skills. *Zero to Three* 14 (5): 15–19.

Howes, C. 1999. Attachment relationships in the context of multiple caregivers. In *Handbook of attachment theory and research,* eds. J. Cassidy & P.R. Shaver, 671–87. New York: Guilford.

Howes, C., C. Rodning, D. Galluzzo, & L. Myers. 1988. Attachment and child care. *Early Childhood Research Quarterly* 3: 401–16.

Kagan, J. 1982. *Research on the human infant: An evaluation summary.* New York: W.P. Grant Foundation.

Karen, R. 1994. *Becoming attached: Unfolding the mystery of the infant-mother bond and its impact on later life.* New York: Warner.

Kempe, C.H., F.N. Silverman, B. Steele, W. Droegmuller, & H.K. Steele. 1962. The battered child syndrome. *Journal of the American Medical Association* 181: 17–24.

Kestenbaum, C. 1984. Pathological attachments and their relationship to affective disorders in adult life. *American Journal of Psychoanalysis* 44 (1): 33–49.

Koops, W., J.B. Hoeksma, & D.C. van den Boom, eds. 1997. *Development of interaction and attachment: Traditional and non-traditional approaches.* Amsterdam: North Holland.

Lally, J.R., A. Griffin, E. Fenichel, M. Segal, E. Szanton, & B. Weissbourd. 1991. *Caring for infants and toddlers in groups: Developmentally appropriate practice*. Washington, DC: Zero to Three.

Lamb, M.E., ed. 1997. *The role of the father in child development*. 3d ed. New York: Wiley.

Lamb, M.E., J.H. Pleck, & J.A. Levine. 1985. The role of the father in child development: The effects of increased paternal involvement. In *Advances in clinical child psychology*, vol. 8, eds. A.B.B. Lahey & A.E. Kazden, 229–66. New York: Plenum.

Main, M., & R. Goldwyn. In press. Interview-based adult attachment classifications: Related to infant-mother and infant-father attachment.

Main, M., N. Kaplan, & J. Cassidy. 1985. Security in infancy, childhood, and adulthood: A move to the level of representation. In *Growing points of attachment theory and research*, eds. I. Bretherton & E. Waters, 66–104. Monographs of the Society for Research in Child Development, vol. 50, nos. 1–2, serial no. 209. Chicago: University of Chicago Press.

Main, M., & J. Solomon. 1990. Procedures for identifying infants as disorganized/disoriented during the Ainsworth Strange Situation. In *Attachment in the preschool years*, eds. M.T. Greenberg, D. Cicchetti, & E.M. Cummings, 87–160. Chicago: University of Chicago Press.

Main, M., & D.R. Weston. 1981. The quality of the toddler's relationship to mother and to father related to conflict behavior and readiness to establish new relationships. *Child Development* 52: 932–40.

Marsiglio, W., P. Amato, R.D. Day, & M.E. Lamb. 2000. Scholarship on fatherhood in the 1990s and beyond. *Journal of Marriage and the Family* 62 (4): 1173–91.

Matas, L., R.A. Arend, & L.A. Sroufe. 1978. Continuity of adaptation in the second year: The relationship between quality of attachment and later competence. *Child Development* 19: 547–56.

Miller, L.G., & K.M. Albrecht. 2000. *Innovations: The comprehensive infant curriculum*. Beltsville, MD: Gryphon House.

Moore, G.A., J.F. Cohn, J. Belsky, & S.B. Campbell. 1996. A comparison of traditional and quantitative classification of attachment status. *Infant Behavior and Development* 19: 265–68.

NICHD Early Child Care Research Network. 1997. The effects of infant child care on infant-mother attachment security: Results of the NICHD Study of Early Child Care. *Child Development* 68 (5): 860–79.

NICHD Early Child Care Research Network. 2001. Early child care and children's development prior to school entry. Paper presented at the symposium, Most Recent Findings from the NICHD Study of Early Child Care. Biennial Meeting of the Society for Research in Child Development, 19 April, in Minneapolis, Minnesota.

Noppe, I.C., J.G. Elicker, & C. Fortner-Wood. 1998. Stability, concordance and correlations of attachment security for infants in child care centers. Poster presentation at the 11th Biennial International Conference on Infant Studies, April, in Atlanta, Georgia.

Park, K., & A.S. Honig. 1991. Infant child care patterns and later teacher ratings of preschool behaviors. *Early Child Development and Care* 68: 89–96.

Peth-Pierce, R. 1998. *The NICHD Study of Early Child Care.* NIH pub. no. 98-4318. Washington, DC: U.S. Department of Health and Human Resouces.

Pierrehumbert, B., R. Miljkovitch, B. Plancherel, O. Halfon, & F. Ansermet. 2000. Attachment and temperament in early childhood: Implications for later behavior problems. *Infant and Child Development* 9: 17–32.

Pitzer, R.L., & J.E. Hessler. 1992. What do we know about fathers? In *Working with fathers: Methods and perspectives,* ed. Minnesota Fathering Alliance. Stillwater, MN: Nu Ink Unlimited. [out of print]

Raikes, H. 1993. Relationship duration in infant care: Time with a high-ability teacher and infant-teacher attachment. *Early Childhood Research Quarterly* 8: 309–25.

Ramsburg, D. 1998. Separation anxiety in young children. *NPIN* [National Parent Information Network] *Parent News* 4 (8). Available online: http://npin.org/pnews/1989/pnew898/inte898a.html (28 January 2002).

Schneider-Rosen, K., K.G. Braunwald, V. Carlson, & D. Cicchetti. 1985. Current perspectives in attachment theory: Illustration from the study of maltreated infants. In *Growing points of attachment theory and research,* eds. I. Bretherton & E. Waters, 194–210. Monographs of the Society for Research in Child Development, vol. 50, nos. 1–2, serial no. 209. Chicago: University of Chicago Press.

Shore, R. 1997. *Rethinking the brain: New insights into early development.* New York: Families and Work Institute.

Solomon, J., & C. George. 1999. *Attachment and disorganization.* New York: Guilford.

Sroufe, L.A. 1979. The coherence of individual development: Early care, attachment, and subsequent developmental issues. *American Psychologist* 34 (10): 834–41.

Sroufe, L.A. 1983. Infant-caregiver attachment and patterns of adaptation in the preschool: The roots of competence and maladaptation. Vol. 16 in *The Minnesota symposia in child psychology*, ed. M. Perlmutter, 41–83. Hillsdale, NJ: Erlbaum.

Sroufe, L.A. 1989. Relationships and relationship disturbances. In *Relationship disturbances in early childhood*, eds. A.J. Sameroff & R.N. Emde, 97–124. New York: Basic.

Sroufe, L.A., & J. Fleeson. 1986. Attachment and the construction of relationships. In *Relationships and development*, eds. W.W. Hartup & Z. Rubin, 51–71. Hillsdale, NJ: Erlbaum.

Sroufe, L.A., & J. Fleeson. 1988. The coherence of family relationships. In *Relationships within families: Mutual influences*, eds. R.A. Hinde & J. Stevenson-Hinde. Oxford, UK: Clarendon.

Stayton, D.J., R. Hogan, & M.D.S. Ainsworth. 1971. Infant obedience and maternal behavior: The origins of socialization reconsidered. *Child Development* 42 (4): 1057–69

Steele, M., H. Steele, & P. Fonagy. 1996. Associations among attachment classifications of mothers, fathers, and their infants. *Child Development* 67: 541–55.

Stevenson-Hinde, J. 1990. Attachment within family systems: An overview. *Infant Mental Health Journal* 11: 218–27.

Stevenson-Hinde, J. 1991. Temperament and attachment: An eclectic approach. In *The development and the integration of behavior*, ed. P. Bateson, 315–29. Cambridge, UK: Cambridge University Press.

Stone, J. 1973a. *Day care for kibbutz toddlers.* Tuckahoe, NY: Campus Film Distributors. Film.

Stone, J. 1973b. *Rearing kibbutz babies.* Tuckahoe, NY: Campus Film Distributors. Film.

Thomas, A., S. Chess, & H. Birch. 1968. *Temperament and behavior disorders in children.* New York: International Universities Press.

Troy, M., & L.A. Sroufe. 1987. Victimization among preschoolers: The role of attachment relationship history. *Journal of the American Academy of Child Psychiatry* 26: 166–72.

Turner, P.J. 1991. Relations between attachment, gender, and behavior with peers in preschool. *Child Development* 62: 1475–88.

van den Boom, D.C. 1994. The influence of temperament and mothering on attachment and exploration: An experimental manipulation of sensitive responsiveness among lower-class mothers with irritable infants. *Child Development* 65: 1457–77.

van den Boom, D.C. 1997. Sensitivity and attachment: Next steps for developmentalists. *Child Development* 68: 592–94.

van IJzendoorn, M., & M.S. De Wolff. 1997. In search of the absent father—Meta-analyses of infant-father attachment: A rejoinder to our discussants. *Child Development* 68 (4): 604–09.

Vaughn, B.E., K.E. Deane, & E. Waters. 1985. The impact of out-of-home care on child-mother attachment quality: Another look at some enduring questions. In *Growing points of attachment theory and research,* eds. I. Bretherton & E. Waters, 110–46. Monographs of the Society for Research in Child Development, vol. 50, nos. 1–2, serial no. 209. Chicago: University of Chicago Press.

Vygotsky, L.S. [1930–1935] 1978. *Mind in society: The development of higher mental processes,* eds. & trans. M. Cole, V. John-Steiner, S. Scribner, & E. Souberman. Cambridge, MA: Harvard University Press.

Werner, E.E. 1993. Risk, resilience, and recovery—Perspectives from the Kauai Longitudinal Study. *Development and Psychopathology* 5 (Fall): 503–15.

Wittmer, D.S., & A.S. Honig. 1987. Do boy toddlers bug teachers more? *Canadian Children* 12 (1): 21–27.

Zaslow, M., & C. Hayes. 1986. Sex differences in children's responses to psychosocial stress: Toward a cross-context analysis. In *Advances in developmental psychology,* vol. 4, eds. M. Lamb & B. Rogoff, 289–337. Hillsdale, NJ: Erlbaum.

Zeanah, C.H., & P.D. Zeanah. 1989. Intergenerational transmission of maltreatment: Insights from attachment theory and research. *Psychiatry* 52: 177–96.